JOHN PAUL II

A Pilgrim on the Roads of the World

Celebrating 25 Years of the Paradigm of Assisi
Assisi 1986 - Assisi 2011

JOHN PAUL II

A Pilgrim on the Roads of the World

Celebrating 25 Years of the Paradigm of Assisi
Assisi 1986 - Assisi 2011

Teresa Joseph fma

2011

John Paul II : *A Pilgrim on the Roads of the World* —Published by the Rev. Dr. Ashish Amos of the Indian Society for Promoting Christian Knowledge (ISPCK), Post Box 1585, 1654, Madarsa Road, Kashmere Gate, Delhi-110006.

© Author, 2011

All rights reserved. No part of this book may be reproduced or transmitted in any form or by any means, electronic, mechanical, photocopying, recording, or by any information storage and retrieval system, without the prior permission in writing from the publisher.

The views expressed in the book are those of the author and the publisher takes no responsibility for any of the statements.

ISBN: 978-81-8465-196-6

Laser typeset by

ISPCK, Post Box 1585, 1654, Madarsa Road, Kashmere Gate, Delhi-110006 • *Tel:* 23866323/22

e-mail: ashish@ispck.org.in • ella@ispck.org.in
website: www.ispck.org.in

Contents

CHAPTER ONE

**"Pilgrimage" as Mysticism of the Crowd in the
"Liminal Period" Between Two Popes**

CHAPTER TWO

**John Paul II: A Pontiff in Dialogue with the Young
and their Educators**   36

CHAPTER THREE
The Paradigm of Assisi   55

CHAPTER FOUR
A Practical Approach to the Paradigm of Assisi   66

Foreword

First of all, I wish to congratulate Sister Teresa Joseph fma for her timely contribution to inter-religious dialogue. This book comes as we all prepare for the great event that will take place next October 2011 in Assisi. Pope Benedict XVI has announced this event to commemorate XXV Years of the Day of Prayer and Fast, which took place on 27 October 1986 at the instance of Blessed John Paul II. It was a singular and an unrepeatable event; however, the spirit of that event needs to be continued because peace is not a one-time achievement. It needs to be continually built and vigilantly preserved.

The World Day of Prayer for Peace has been an open-ended event; its spirit intends to encourage further initiatives to build bridges of friendship across religious boundaries on local and grass-roots levels throughout the world in order to inspire "culture of dialogue and peace." It is meant to be a "world movement of prayer for peace" because "peace is a universal responsibility: it comes about through a thousand little acts in daily life. By their daily way of living with others, people choose for or against peace." Addressing the leaders of different religions on 29 October 1986, Blessed John Paul II shared his intention with them. He said to them, "Let us continue to live the Spirit of Assisi." With these challenging words, Blessed John Paul II invited the religious leaders, who participated in the World Day of Prayer for Peace, to "recognise their responsibilities and recommit themselves to the task of peace, to put into action the strategies of peace with courage and vision."[1]

"Spirit of Assisi" should not be imagined as a vague activity that might be undertaken by people who engage in inter-religious relations. "Spirit of Assisi" needs to be carefully grasped and meticulously followed so that not even the idea of religious relativism or syncretism, is brought to the minds of believers. While "Spirit of Assisi" encourages genuine and serious dialogue among religions, relativism and syncretism should be considered as archenemies of that dialogue. Blessed John Paul II himself, two months after the Day of Prayer for peace in Assisi, explained the meaning, the limitation and the possible path to continue the "Spirit of Assisi." In his address on 22 December 1986, Blessed John Paul II reflected deeper on the event of Assisi. He said to the Members of the Roman Curia: "It is indeed obvious that we cannot remain content with the fact itself and its successful realisation. It is certain that the Day of Assisi urges all whose personal and community life is guided by a conviction of faith to draw its consequences in a deeper understanding of peace and of a new way of committing oneself to peace. Apart from this, and perhaps in the very first place, the day invites us to an "exegesis" of what happened at Assisi and of its intimate meaning, in the light of our Christian and Catholic faith. The appropriate key to interpret such a great event derives from the teaching of the Second Vatican Council, which in a breathtaking way associates rigorous fidelity to the biblical revelation and to the tradition of the Church with awareness of the needs and the anxieties of our times, expressed in such eloquent "signs" (cf. GS, n. 4). The event of Assisi can

---

[1] John Paul II, Concluding Address, 27 October 1986.

thus be considered as a visible illustration, an exegesis of the events, a catechesis, intelligible to all, of what is presupposed and signified by the commitment to ecumenism and to inter-religious dialogue, which was recommended and promoted by the Second Vatican Council."

In the same address of 22 December 1986, Blessed John Paul II dwelt on themes, such as the unity of the origin and goal of the human family, differences among religions, mission of the Church and identity of the Catholic Church. The situation of the world since 1986 has become worse and peace is more difficult to find. Is it not urgent that believers of all religions pay heed to the prophetic call of Blessed Pope John Paul II, which "is itself a dramatic appeal to rediscover and keep always alive the Spirit of Assisi, as a motive of hope for the future"?

The success of the World Day of Prayer for Peace in Assisi in 1986 and its inspiring memory after twenty-five years is a proof that the vast number of the population of the world ardently longs for peace. This ardent longing is evident in the profound desire of religious believers to pray for peace. The event in 1986 unequivocally affirmed that peace is impossible without prayer. As our world is increasingly becoming multi-religious, this desire among believers to pray for peace is seen on the increase and is obviously being expressed in small or large, formal or informal inter-religious gatherings. In the light of the Sacred Scriptures and the Christian tradition, we must affirm that "every authentic prayer is under the influence of the Spirit 'who intercedes insistently for us... because we do not even know how to pray as we ought', but He prays in us 'with unutterable groanings' and 'the One who searches hearts knows what are the desires of the Spirit' (cf. Rom 8:26-27). We can indeed maintain that every authentic prayer is called forth by the Holy Spirit, who is mysteriously present in the heart of every person." However, experience teaches us that this desire to pray in inter-religious gatherings must not give the believers at large a mixed and a confused message that "one religion is as good as the other" or that "fundamentally different religions can be reduced just to one." If that were to happen, it would be the end, not only of inter-religious dialogue, but above all of religion itself. Although believers have a single goal and a shared intention, namely peace, utmost care must be taken when believers come together to pray, so that one another's religious traditions are respected. "In this too, deep down, there is a message: we wish to show the world that the genuine impulse to prayer does not lead to opposition and still less to disdain of others, but rather to constructive dialogue, a dialogue in which each one, without relativism or syncretism of any kind, becomes more deeply aware of the duty to bear witness and to proclaim."[2]

Of the several initiatives undertaken to continue the "Spirit of Assisi", a mention could be made of two: Sant'Egidio Community in Rome has been organising every year inter-religious gathering called "People and Religions" (*Uomini e Religioni*). It brings together people of different religions from around the world to reflect on themes of actuality and of common concern. This annual event gives the followers of different religions an occasion to manifest to the world at large that "believers of all religions stand with one voice and readily collaborate to bring peace in our world." Blessed John Paul II expressed his happiness that the "Spirit of Assisi" has been continuing: "The pilgrimage of peace, which began with the historical event of Assisi in October 1986, has already passed

---

[2] John Paul II, 24 January 2002, n.7.

through many cities of Europe and the Mediterranean area, involving representatives of different religious denominations. Now it is experiencing a further significant stage. In Assisi, at the close of a memorable day, the invitation to continue on the journey of seeking peace, "the path on which we must walk together" arose naturally. I am happy to see that the journey then started continues, and that it increasingly attracts men and women of different religions and cultures, all united in the sole desire for the great gift of peace."[3]

The event in Assisi in 1986 has also been the source of inspiration to a group of Buddhists in Japan. The late Venerable Yamada, who at the age of over eighty years, had participated in the Day of Prayer for Peace in Assisi in 1986. Upon his return to Japan, he organised an inter-religious event in August 1987 on Mount Hiei near Kyoto. Coinciding with the memory of the Hiroshima bombings on 6 August, the "Spirit of Assisi" continues and people gather every year to pray for peace. It is heartening to know that next year this initiative will complete twenty-five years.

Blessed John Paul II, wished that "Spirit of Assisi" be passed on to the new generations. He wrote: "We must foster the genuine 'Spirit of Assisi' not only out of duty to be consistent and faithful, but also in order to offer reason for hope to future generations."[4] It is in the hope to continue the "Spirit of Assisi" that the Pontifical Council for Inter-religious Dialogue organised an inter-religious youth meeting in Assisi from 4-8 November 2006. While the inter-religious youth meeting was meant to commemorate the XXth anniversary of the World Day

---

[3] Letter to Cardinal Cassidy for the International Encounter of Prayer held in Milan, September 16, 1993.

[4] John Paul II, Message for the World Day of Peace, December 8, 1991.

of Prayer for Peace in Assisi in 1986, the organisers also hoped to pass on the "Spirit of Assisi" to today's youth, many of whom were not yet born or were yet infants when the *religious event that attracted the greatest attention in the world*" took place in Assisi in 1986.

At the dawn of the new millennium, Blessed Pope John Paul II exhorted: "[A relationship of openness and dialogue with the followers of other religions] must continue. In the climate of increased cultural and religious pluralism, which is expected to make the society of the new millennium, it is obvious that this dialogue will be especially important in establishing a sure basis for peace and warding off the dread spectre of those wars of religion which have so often bloodied human history. The name of the one God must become increasingly what it is: *a name of peace and a summons to peace.*[5]"

The appalling events that shook the world at the very beginning of the third millennium sowed seeds of violence and hatred and broke the spell of a society that saw itself as advanced and free, but in an instant found itself fragile, divided and threatened. The terrorist acts of 11 September 2001 in the United States of America and subsequent similar events in other parts of the world, especially in India, shook the hearts of everyone, shattered hope and revealed the weakness of the world situation. There was a danger that these events would be seen as a conflict between economic and social systems or, worse still, as a clash between the Muslim world and other religions, especially Christianity.

---

[5] John Paul II, Novo Millennio Ineunte, n. 55.

It is in the context of the precarious character of our world that the significance of the daring and prophetic gesture of Blessed John Paul II must be understood. His successor, Pope Benedict XVI, in his address to the Bishop of Assisi on 2 September 2006 reminded everyone that, "(Pope John Paul II's) invitation to the world's religious leaders to bear a unanimous witness to peace serves to explain with no possibility of confusion that *religion must be a herald of peace.*"[6] Pope Benedict XVI further recognises in the World Day of Prayer for Peace in Assisi in 1986 the religious sense having reached "maturity" which gave "rise to a perception in the believer that *faith in God, Creator of the universe and Father of all, must encourage relations of universal brotherhood among human beings.*"[7] People of goodwill throughout the world have welcomed the initiative of Pope Benedict XVI to convoke religious leaders in Assisi next October to pray for world peace. May Sister Teresa Joseph's book help and guide many people to organise concurring events in every part of the world as Pope Benedict XVI meets religious leaders in Assisi to commemorate 25 Years of the Day of Prayer and Fast in Assisi.

May initiatives be multiplied throughout the world to diffuse a "culture of dialogue." Here again, Blessed John Paul II, on the eve of the Great Jubilee of the Year 2000, declared to the religious leaders: "The task before us therefore is to promote a culture of dialogue. Individually and together, we must show how religious belief inspires peace, encourages solidarity, promotes justice and upholds liberty."[8]

---

[6] Benedict XVI, For the XX anniversary : Interreligious Prayer Meeting for Peace, Assisi, 2 September 2006.

[7] *Ibid.,*

[8] John Paul II, to the participants in Interreligious Assembly, 28 October 1999.

May the symbol of Assisi, as a ray of hope, continue to remain strong in the memory of all people, and may the "Spirit of Assisi" as a ray of light continue to illumine the world that is marked by the darkness of hatred and violence.

+ Archbishop Felix Machado

Vasai, India,

Feast of Mary, Help of Christians

24 May 2011

Introduction

The beatification of Pope John Paul II and the forthcoming 25th anniversary of his "Prayer for Peace" encounter in Assisi provided splendid opportunities to revisit our "Beloved Pope", a true pilgrim on the roads of the world. "Pilgrimage—going on a sacred journey"—is one of the characteristics of the human family. In all religions, pilgrimage is a fundamental dimension of a faith journey. Pilgrimages, either the so-called traditional or local, have a certain pattern of experience and expression.

Victor Turner has explored in depth the concept of pilgrimage. His work on African, Mexican, Muslim, Christian and other pilgrimage traditions has brought to light a variety of shared characteristics of pilgrimages in spite of the many differences. The striking metaphor of "pilgrimage" is one of the connecting links between believers of various religions.

The pages of this book need to be placed therefore on the vast horizon of the Church in her mission of dialogue and search together with the believers of other religions for the "ray of that truth which enlightens all men" and at the same time convinced of and accompanied by an equally firm exposition of the ecclesial faith.

This book consists of four chapters. The first chapter takes the reader to the heart of pilgrimage and John Paul II's insights into pilgrimage. Religious pluralism and education to proclaim, defend and spread the truth and a precious methodology for inter-religious dialogue are some of the topics dealt with in the second chapter. According to Zelindo Trenti, "religious education is committed to reawaken and to refine a contemplative attitude."[1] Contemplation leads to mysticism.

The field of education is one of the most captivating and rewarding fields that offer space to try out new possibilities. Entering into the dynamic of treasuring the personal patrimony of believers of each religion, for the benefit of the community, there is need to translate into practical level theological and dogmatic ideas. This can offer possibilities of collaboration at a larger level with different categories of persons.

The third chapter focuses on the memorable "Prayer for Peace" encounter in Assisi called for by Pope John Paul II in 1986. The paradigmatic metaphor of Assisi, St. Peter's Square, Rome, a replica of Assisi and contemplation and the power that leads to dialogue are the topics that find their right place in this chapter.

Assisi 1986 is not going to remain as an isolated event. To commemorate the 25th anniversary of Pope John Paul II's "Prayer for Peace" encounter in Assisi, Pope Benedict XVI, and leaders of other Christian communities and representatives of the world's major religions will gather in Assisi in October 2011. "The 1986 event was seen by many as a milestone in inter-religious relations but was criticised by some Catholics who

---

[1] Zelindo Trenti , *Educare alla fede – saggio di pedagogia religiosa*, Elledici, Leumann (Torino) 2000, 106-107. Walter·Brueggmann, *Living Toward a Vision: Biblical Reflections on Shalom*, New York, United Church Press, 1982, 16.

said it appeared to inappropriately mix elements from Christian and non-Christian religions."[2]

The Vatican press office issued a statement giving the theme for the 2011 event: "Pilgrims of Truth, Pilgrims of Peace"— and a general outline of events. The statement said Pope Benedict will prepare for the Assisi gathering by hosting a prayer service with Catholics from the Diocese of Rome in St Peter's Basilica the evening before.

The Pontiff and representatives of the world's major religions "will make speeches and sign a common commitment to peace when they meet in Assisi in October, but they will not pray together, the Vatican has said."

"Every human being is ultimately a pilgrim in search of truth and goodness," the Vatican statement said. In their search for truth, people enter into dialogue with each other. It is important that the dialogue is carried out respecting each one's identity and without indulging in forms of syncretism. "To the extent that the pilgrimage of truth is authentically lived, it opens the path to dialogue with the other, it excludes no one and it commits everyone to be a builder of fraternity and peace. These are the elements that the Holy Father wishes to place at the centre of reflection," the Vatican said.

The extraordinary meetings at Assisi are a strong source of inspiration to create a new way of thinking and acting. The fourth chapter offers practical guidelines on how to make the paradigm of Assisi enhance the lives of educators, students and all those interested in committing themselves to promote peace and harmony. It is a concrete effort to translate into

---

[2] Source: *Catholic News Service dated.*

pastoral action the "diakonia of the truth" as a new style of pedagogy of inter-religious dialogue. Today, in the midst of terrorism and religious intolerance, we need to multiply the experience of Assisi. The sessions will receive colour and vivacity depending on the sensibility and openness of the educators to enter into inter-religious dialogue in the spirit of truth and love.

CHAPTER ONE

"Pilgrimage" as Mysticism of the Crowd in the "Liminal Period" Between Two Popes

Courtesy ISPCK Delhi[1]

The Anthropological Basis of Pilgrimage

Karol Wojtyla (1920-2005) - John Paul II (1978-2005)

The passing away of Pope John Paul II on Saturday 2 April 2005 and the crowds of pilgrims that poured into St. Peter's Square, Rome, is a strong invitation to reflect on breaking new grounds in pilgrimage. The beautiful metaphor of "pilgrimage", which describes the individual and communitarian human condition in Turner, in the texts of Vatican II and even more in the encyclical *Fides et ratio* of John Paul II, found an eloquent explosion in the "Universal pilgrimage to say thanks to the Pilgrim."[2]

---

[1] This chapter forms part of the book *Family of Truth: The Liminal Context of Inter-Religious Dialogue An Anthropological and Pedagogical Enquiry,* ISPCK, Delhi, 549-568. We are grateful to Rev. Ashish Amos, General Secretary of ISPCK, for permitting us to use this chapter in this book. Permission was received through the e-mal message dated 13 March 2011.

[2] *Un pellegrinaggio universale per dire grazie al Pellegrino* in *L'Osservatore Romano,* Mercoledì 6 april 2005, 1.

Victor Turner and Edith Turner have highlighted how for many the pilgrimage was the great liminal experience of one's life. They stressed two types of pilgrimages: interior and exterior. In the monasteries, the contemplatives and mystics could daily carry out saving interior journeys. The ordinary people had to externalise their journeys in the common adventure of pilgrimage. Against this background, it is not difficult to grasp the profound significance of Turner's affirmation, "If mysticism is an interior pilgrimage, pilgrimage is exteriorized mysticism."[3]

The mystical experience can be examined from the psychological, philosophical-dialogical, and religious perspective. Now, a new and unexpected challenge meets us: Why not consider "pilgrimage as mysticism of the crowd in the liminal period between two Popes."

Turner has cited the communitarian dimension of rites and beliefs. Exploring this concept further, one realises how for him the rites and beliefs are intrinsically involved with the social process of the entire community. For this reason, "religion is the motor of social life."[4]

Turner knew when he borrowed the term from Martin Buber that communitas is typified by the kind of I-Thou relationship existing paradigmatically between God and creature. Turner affirmed that it is the sacrality of social life that renders it intelligible. He razed the wall between text based or theologically based religious studies and the social sciences by resituating social sacrality within individual experience. For Turner the religious persons who pass in and out of all 'arenas' and 'theaters' are the strands from which communal

---

[3] Victor Turner, Edith Turner, *Image and Pilgrimage in Christian Culture, Anthropological perspectives*, New York, Columbia University Press, 1978. 7.

[4] Victor Turner, *Ritual, Tribal and Catholic*, in *Worship* 50 (1976) 508.

life is woven. He took his dictum from William Blake's
Jerusalem: 'General Forms have their vitality in particulars
and every particular is a man'.[5]

It is an anthropological and phenomenological approach that
will facilitate a fruitful understanding of pilgrimage as
mysticism of the crowd. Such an approach has to respect the
anthropology common to all. It is this anthropology that unites
the human family and recognises that there will always be
doctrinal differences among religions. This is thinkable only
in the light of the Holy Spirit. Moved by the Holy Spirit in this
way in the encounter between members of various religions,
we can foresee the design of God to unite all peoples. Such
encounters have characteristics that are typica : the search for
truth and genuine commitment to share at the common table
the elements of truth already found. This means to enthuse in
the educating community people who are open and who allow
themselves be lead by the Holy Spirit and to anthropological
places in which the religious phenomenon grows and bears
fruit.

Wojtyla's dissertation on "An Evaluation of the Possibility
of Constructing a Christian Ethics on the Basis of the System
of Max Scheler" analysed Scheler's phenomenology with a view
to assessing its value for Catholic thought. This helped him to
appreciate the valid contribution of phenomenology to
understand the human experience.

> He insisted that it would end in solipsism if not grounded in
> 'a general theory of things-as-they-are.' The study marked
> Wojtyla's attempt to link the objectivity of philosophy with
> the subjectivity of individual experience, and it manifested
> his characteristic tendency to reconcile or connect apparently

---

[5] Lawrence E. Sullivan, *Victor Turner, 1920-1983* in *History of Religions*
24 (1984) 2, 163.

opposing aspects of thought and experience, as in his book, *Love and Responsibility*, which appeared in 1960.[6]

The communitarian dimension in the experience of God shines in the gaze of a believer. This is an experience that is very intimate and personal. The pedagogical process of this encounter-dialogue among these two partners is interpreted and expressed through the multiplicity and plurality of cultures of the human family. The inter-disciplinary dialogue that highlights the style of relationship between God and the human person requires an undisturbed communication and exchange between the lovers of the science of religions and the representatives and scholars of different religious experiences and traditions. Attention has to be focused on the eruption of the sacred and the welcoming of it on the part of people in individual socio-cultural contexts. A key to reading in order to verify the authenticity of religious experience is found in the anthropological openness expressed through an attitude of acceptance on the part of people, which, in the final analysis, is a gratuitous gift and a free response. This is expressed in all its creativity in the transparency of the anthropological subject. A splendid field to be explored in this direction is the pedagogical one, where educators as believers of various religions are committed to find ways to allow the face of the divine to shine through the texts and in classrooms.

An Immense Crowd of Pilgrims

Neither the Paul VI Hall nor the St. Peter's Square was sufficient to accommodate the pilgrims who poured into Rome after receiving the news of the passing away of the Pope. *L'Osservatore Romano* of 7 April beautifully described this

---

[6] Elizabeth Fox Genovese, *The Legacy of John Paul II. Why the bishop of Rome may be the most important figure in this secularistic age* in *http://www.ctlibrary.com/268* (accessed on 12/4/2005).

reality: "Un popolo immenso di pellegrini continua l'omaggio a Giovanni Paolo II: è un incontro che ha come aula il mondo e come uditorio l'intera umanità" [7] (An immense crowd of pilgrims continue to pay their homage to John Paul II: it is an encounter that has the world as a hall and the entire humanity as its audience). John Paul II catechised without words. It is a meeting of hearts, and words give way to contemplation. It is a prolonged dialogue between the Father and the children. Of course, it is an "unpublished" dialogue where the mysticism of the crowd, thanks to the mysticism of John Paul II, exploded in praise and in joyful clapping. In this context, faith shines out in the very attitude of the pilgrims.

For John Paul II, death, of course, was the final pilgrimage into the Father's home. But for the human family, this great pilgrimage of his is a historical moment to express both affection and gratitude for his love for each person. It is a splendid occasion to assure him that "humanity is in 'spiritual journey' with John Paul II."[8] With 104 "officially registered" apostolic journeys: from the one to San Domingo and Mexico in January 1979 to that to Lourdes in 2004, John Paul II has travelled widely and gone out of his way to make visible God's love for the human family.

---

[7] L'Osservatore Romano, Giovedì 7 aprile 2005, 1. See also *Ibid., Lo straordinario e ininterrotto pellegrinaggio di cuori per rendere omaggio al Papa nella Basilica Vaticana*, Servizi di Gianfranco Grieco di Giampaolo Mattei di Gianluca Biccini e di Niccola Gori, 2-3. Gianfranco Grieco, *"Ho fatto conoscere loro il tuo nome perché l'amore sia in essi"*. Giampaolo Mattei, *Una finestra si è chiusa Una porta si è spalancata*. Gianluca Biccini, *"Unico grande amore" L'omaggio delle nuove generazioni*. Niccola Gori, *Ha radunato i popoli intorno a Cristo e al suo Vangelo*.

[8] Giampaolo Mattei, *L'ultimo e più grande Viaggio Apostolico di Giovanni Paolo II sulla Rotta di Dio* in *L'Osservatore Romano*, Mercoledì 6 april 2005, 3.

John Paul II's Insights on Pilgrimage

Pilgrimage indicates almost a permanent disposition of the human heart. Life is a journey and the concept of pilgrimage is closely connected to the existential situation of the human person. The Church journeys with the pilgrim people in the footsteps of Jesus Christ with the awareness of her dialogical nature.

> From birth to death, the condition of each individual is that of the *homo viator*. [...] The history of the Church is the living account of an unfinished pilgrimage. A pilgrimage evokes the believer's personal journey in the footsteps of the Redeemer: it is an exercise of practical asceticism, of repentance for human weaknesses, of constant vigilance over one's own frailty, of interior preparation for a change of heart.[9]

In the pilgrim journey with the human family, the Church becomes aware of the life of people. The new pedagogy of sharing Christ is born out of a contemplative adoration of the Lord and of the realities of the world. "My Jubilee pilgrimage to the *Holy Places* brought me to the land that saw the birth, life, death and resurrection of Jesus Christ and the beginning of the Church. [...] It was a return, in a sense, to the origins, to the roots of our faith and of the Church."[10]

John Paul II, besides his daily pilgrimage that was his own personal journey in the footsteps of the Redeemer, journeyed into the human family making its joys and sorrows his own. Like Jesus, he met people in their human condition. He was able to attract crowds of people and to have a penetrating understanding of the social context of Christianity today. He

---

[9] John Paul II, *Papal Bull Incarnationis Mysterium* n.7. in *http:// www.vatican.va/jubilee 2000/ docs/documents/hf jp-ii doc 30111998 bolla- jubilee en.html* (accessed on 8/4/2005).

[10] John Paul II, *General Audience*, Wednesday 29 March 2000.

contemplated the rays of truth present in other religions considering them as positive challenges. He manifested the certainty of a clear identity and, at the same time, was fully open to other peoples, nations and cultures. With his motto, *totus tuus*, he made divine mercy visible on the roads of the world. Even in the midst of shouts of joy, song and dance, he was capable of drawing young and old to prayer, to contemplation and conversion. He knew his role as a Pilgrim among pilgrims.

> The Church is no stranger to this journey of discovery, nor could she ever be. From the moment when, through the Paschal Mystery, she received the gift of the ultimate truth about human life, the Church has made her pilgrim way along the paths of the world to proclaim that Jesus Christ is "the way, and the truth, and the life" (*Jn* 14:6). It is her duty to serve humanity in different ways, but one way in particular imposes a responsibility of a quite special kind: the *diakonia of the truth*. FR2

John Paul II, through his pontificate, has left to the Church a rich heritage of being "a partner in humanity's shared struggle to arrive at truth" and "to proclaim the certitudes arrived at, albeit with a sense that every truth attained is but a step towards that fullness of truth which will appear with the final Revelation of God." FR2

John Paul II stressed how the Great Jubilee has to be lived as a great interior experience. In the introduction to his letter "concerning pilgrimage to the places linked to the History of Salvation", he wrote:

> The Great Jubilee is not just a series of functions to be held, but a great interior experience to be lived. External factors make sense only in so far as they express a deeper commitment which touches people's hearts. It was in fact this inner dimension that I wished to point out to everyone in my Apostolic Letter *Tertio Millennio Adveniente* and the Jubilee

Bull of Indiction *Incarnationis Mysterium*, both of which were well received by a great many people.[11]

His own special Jubilee pilgrimage to the places closely linked to the Incarnation of the Word of God, the event which the Holy Year of 2000 directly recalled, indeed, could be understood fully only in the light of the above.

I have a strong desire to go personally to pray in the most important places which, from the Old to the New Testament, have seen God's interventions, which culminate in the mysteries of the Incarnation and of the Passion, Death and Resurrection of Christ. These places are already indelibly etched in my memory; from the time when in 1965 I had the opportunity to visit the Holy Land. It was an unforgettable experience. Today I still gladly go back to what I wrote then, pages full of emotion.

I come across these places which you have filled with yourself once and for all. ... Oh place ... You were transformed so many times before you, His place, became mine. When for the first time He filled you, you were not yet an outer place; you were but His Mother's womb. How I long to know that the stones I am treading in Nazareth are the same which her feet touched when she was Your only place on earth. Meeting You through the stone touched by the feet of Your Mother. Oh, corner of the earth, place in the holy land – what kind of place are you in me? My steps cannot tread on you; I must kneel. Thus I confirm today you were indeed a place of meeting. Kneeling down I imprint a seal on you. You will remain here with my seal – you will remain – and I will take you and transform you within me into the place of new testimony. I will walk away as a witness who testifies across the millennia (Karol Wojtyla, *Poezje. Poems*, Wydawnictwo Literackie, Kraków 1998, p. 168). [12]

---

[11] John Paul II, *Concerning pilgrimage to the places linked to the History of Salvation, in http:// www.vatican.va/holy father/John Paul II/letters/ documents/hf jp-ii let 30061999 pilgrimage en.html* (accessed on 14/4/2005).

[12] *Ibid.*, n.4.

The Pope wanted his pilgrimage to be a religious one, though spiritually he was already on this journey.

> It would be an exclusively religious pilgrimage in its nature and purpose, and I would be saddened if anyone were to attach other meanings to this plan of mine. Indeed, spiritually I am already on this journey, since even to go just in thought to those places means in a way to read anew the Gospel itself; it means to follow the roads which Revelation itself has taken.[13]

In this religious pilgrimage, the Pope had a great desire to be welcomed as a "pilgrim and a brother", to be a messenger of unity among the other churches in the Holy Land.

> More than any other pilgrimage which I have made, the one I am about to undertake in the Holy Land during the Jubilee event will be marked by the desire expressed in Christ's prayer to the Father that his disciples "may all be one" (*Jn* 17:21), a prayer which challenges us more vigorously at the exceptional time which opens the Third Millennium. [...], And I would be happy if we could gather together in the places of our common origin, to bear witness to Christ our unity (cf. *Ut Unum Sint*, 23) and to confirm our mutual commitment to the restoration of full communion.[14]

The pilgrimage of the Pope to the Holy Land and to the various parts of the world was a clear indicator of the pastoral renewal that was taking shape in the Church, in a Church that wants to accompany humanity, supporting modernity in all its positive aspects, and at the same time, a Church ever attentive to speak where human rights and the right to life are in danger or are not respected.

---

[13] *Ibid.,* n.10.

[14] *Ibid.,* n.11.

A Mystic and a Contemplative in Communication with Crowds of People

As head of the Universal Church, John Paul II had a charism for connecting with large crowds, especially with young people. He knew how to blend the monastic mysticism of St. John of the Cross with a professional ability to communicate with immense crowds of people. His thirst to discover the profound mysticism contained in the simplicity of the rosary is a significant example of how he was attentive to prayers dear to popular tradition. For John Paul II, the rosary is a contemplative prayer.[15]

> The Rosary mystically transports us to Mary's side as she is busy watching over the human growth of Christ in the home of Nazareth. This enables her to train us and to mould us with the same care, until Christ is "fully formed" in us (cf. *Gal* 4:19).[16]

Wojtyla was attracted to mysticism from his youth. He was introduced to the writings of Saint John of the Cross by Jan Tyranowski. For his doctoral dissertation, he chose the Spanish Carmelite mystic, St. John of the Cross.[17]

> I myself have been especially attracted by the experience and teachings of the Saint of Fontiveros. From the first years of my priestly formation, I found in him a sure guide in the ways of faith. This aspect of his doctrine seemed to me to be of vital importance to every Christian, especially in a trail-blazing age like our own, which is also filled with risks and temptations in the sphere of faith.

---

[15] John Paul II, *Apostolic Letter, Rosarium Virginis Mariae*, 16 October, 2002, see nos. 5, 12, 39.

[16] *Ibid.*, n.15.

[17] Cf. Tracey Rowland, *Reading St. John of the Cross with John Paul II*, Notes of a lunchtime talk given at the City Branch on October 3, 2001 in *http://www.cclibrary.org.au/LT JoC JPII.html* (accessed on 11/4/2005).

Europe was still bathed in the afterglow of the celebration of the fourth centenary of the birth of the Carmelite Saint (1542-1942) and rising from its ashes after the dark night of war when, in Rome, I wrote my doctoral thesis in theology on the subject of Faith according to St. John of the Cross (1). In it, I devoted special attention to an analytical discussion of the central affirmation of the Mystical Doctor: Faith is the only proximate and proportionate means for communion with God. Even then I felt that John had not only marshalled solid theological doctrine, but that, above all, he had set forth Christian life in terms of such basic aspects as communion with God, the contemplative dimension of prayer, the strength that apostolic mission derives from life in God, and the creative tension of the Christian life lived in hope.[18]

"Faith is the only proximate and proportionate means for communion with God." This central concept of St. John of the Cross the Mystical Doctor, John Paul II incarnated into his very being. Already during his doctorate, he was able to capture how John had grasped the life of a Christian in terms of a few basic aspects. Communion with God that is nourished with the contemplative dimension of prayer, an apostolic life that is strengthened by the life in God and, above all, a Christian life lived in hope in a creative tension, this is the key to reading the Pontificate of John Paul II in a mystical light. For him, encounter with the living God is the centre of Christian life. At the core of mysticism, there is the gradual getting to know God as a person. Mutual self-giving is the active dynamic in such knowledge. The mysticism of the Pope and that of the crowd embrace each other in this mutual self-giving. He presents St

---

[18] John Paul II, *Master in Faith, Apostolic Letter of His Holiness John Paul II To The Very Reverend Father Felipe Sainz De Baranda Superior General of The Order of The Discalced Brothers of The Blessed Virgin Mary of Mount Carmel on The Occasion of The IV Centenary of The Death of Saint John of The Cross, Doctor of The Church, n.4* in http://www.ewtn.com/ library/ *PAPALDOC/ JPMASTER.HTM Master in Faith,* n.2.

John of the Cross: "As a master or guide on the journey of faith, he brings light, through his example and doctrine, to all those who seek to experience God through contemplation and through self-sacrificing service to their brothers and sisters."[19]

John Paul II highlighted service as a prolongation of contemplative prayer. Quoting the dynamic picture of John of the Cross fully dedicated to a variety of works, he goes straight to the point:

> John shows us that the Christian can find complete fulfilment in the contemplative life. The contemplative does not limit himself to spending long stretches in prayer [...]. His attitude may be summed up by a basic conviction: It is God and God alone that gives value and meaning to every activity. For where God is unknown, nothing is known'.[20]

The Pope acknowledged the universal impact of John of the Cross. He is a guide for those who seek God. "He speaks to all of the truth of God and of the surpassing vocation of man." John Paul II's striking intuition about how John of the Cross responded to his historical context inventing for his time a doctrinal system and pastoral approach to "teaching faith in order to liberate it from perils that would waylay the faithful,"[21] in a way offers insights into his own style of pastoral action. John of the Cross had to respond to those who trusted more in private visions and subjective movements than in the Gospel and the Church. He had to find solutions to the radical unbelief and hardness of heart that prevented people opening themselves to mystery.

> The Mystical Doctor avoids these pitfalls and, through his example and doctrine, helps Christians to make their faith

---

19 *Ibid.*

20 *Ibid.*, n.6.

21 *Ibid.*, n.7.

strong with the very basic qualities of an adult faith which the Second Vatican Council asks of us. It is to be a personal faith which has matured through the experience of communion with God. It is to be a faith that leads to solidarity and commitment which is manifested in moral integrity of life and a readiness to serve. This is the faith that we need and which the Saint of Fontiveros offers us through his personal witness and his perennially relevant teaching.[22]

John Paul II had to face the historical context of communism, of growing materialism, of threats to life, of currents of thought that are contrary to the Gospel values. He played a critical role in the downfall of communism. With prophetic courage, he proposed traditional moral values as an alternative to the growing materialism of the West. The cult of life is one of the challenges that the Church has to face, and the strong tendency is to find the message in that same "life." "Life is salvation, life is God."[23] John Paul II courageously proclaimed the sacredness of life through his teaching. "St. John of the Cross has educated generations of faithful in contemplative prayer"[24] and the Pope was one of the champions among them. Two statements help us to get a taste of John Paul II as a mystic. "The Pope has shown the evangelizing power of a mystic", says Cardinal Julián Herranz.

> The media has given a lot of importance to the Pope's more than 100 trips, and to the thousands of people he has touched through them. They've also focused on the dozens of doctrinal documents he's promulgated. But there is another activity of John Paul II's that doesn't get mentioned often,

---

[22] *Ibid.,* n.7.

[23] Michael Fuss, *Nuovi Salvatori per i tempi nuovi? La ricerca di salvezza nella nuova religiosità* in Piero Coda (a cura) *L'Unico e i molti. La salvezza in Gesù Cristo e la sfida del pluralismo,* Roma, Mursia- Pontificia Università Lateranese, 1997, 42.

[24] John Paul II, *Master in Faith,* n.13.

which is the source of everything else he does: the countless hours that he spends praying before the Blessed Sacrament. What impresses me in my personal dealings with him is his mysticism. He is a man who lives in continuous union with God. He not only is the vicar of Christ, but also wants to make Christ present in his words, his teaching, and his actions. I think that mystical dimension is the source of all his apostolic and missionary energy.[25]

The Pope lived the "Come to me" of Jesus in a unique way. So often the media has focussed on him lost in prayer. We saw him on Good Friday during the Way of the Cross absorbed in prayer.

> The most profound experiences that I had were during the visits to his private chapel after the meal. I was very much struck by the profound sense of prayerfulness of the Holy Father.

> Pope John Paul II is able to so focus on his relationship with God that all other people and sounds and settings are blotted out.

> I came away from those times with a conviction that our Holy Father is truly a mystic. His relationship with the Lord is so total and consuming that to be in his presence when he is at prayer enables one to experience the presence of God.

> That conviction endures within me and I seek to imitate in my own poor way the example of a man of profound prayer. A true mystic in our day.[26]

---

25 Cardinal Julián Herranz, The Pope has shown the evangelizing power of a mystic, Interview in El Pais (with Enric González) in *http://www.opusdei.org/art.php?w=32&p=6565* (accessed on 11/5/2005).

[26] Joseph A. Galante, Lost in Prayer, in *http://batr.org/view/040405.html* (accessed on 11/4/2005). Joseph A. Galante has served as auxiliary bishop of San Antonio (1992), bishop of Beaumont (1994) and coadjutor bishop of Dallas (1999).

An Adoring Silence

John Paul II courageously affirmed: "My contact with representatives of the non-Christian spiritual traditions, particularly those of Asia, has confirmed me in the view that the future of mission depends to a great extent on contemplation."[27] Communion between God and the human person is a dynamic process. God and the human person meet in love. "One draws close to this presence above all by letting oneself be taught an adoring silence, for at the culmination of the knowledge and experience of God is His absolute transcendence. This is reached through the prayerful assimilation of scripture and the liturgy more than by systematic meditation."[28] The Pope affirms that we must confess that we all need this silence. It is a silence that is filled with the "presence of Him who is adored: in theology, so as to exploit fully its own sapiential and spiritual soul; in prayer."[29] Seeing God is such a meaningful encounter that the best image to which it is compared is that of Moses (cf. *Ex* 34:33). The profound experience of seeing God makes the face of the believer so radiant that he or she is obliged to cover it with a veil. Another point the Pontiff stresses is the pastoral consequences of a profound encounter with God, the urgent need to make room for God's presence. Where there is space for God, there is less room for "self-celebration, in preaching, so as not to delude ourselves that it is enough to heap words upon words to attract people to the experience of God in

---

[27] John Paul II, *Encyclical letter Redemptoris Missio* [RM] n. 1-92 (7 December 1990), in *EV*/12 (1992), n.91.

[28] John Paul II, *Orientale Lumen* (to mark the Centenary of *Orientalium Dignitas* of Pope Leo XIII in *http://www.vatican.va/holy father/john paul ii/ apost letters/documents/hf jp-ii apl 02051995 orientale-lumen* en.ml (accessed on 10/4/2005), n.16.

[29] *Ibid.*

commitment, so that we will refuse to be locked in a struggle without love and forgiveness."[30]

The Pontiff was well aware of how very essential prayer and contemplation are for dialogue. "I repeat how important it is to revitalize prayer and contemplation in the process of dialogue. Men and women in the consecrated life can contribute very significantly to inter-religious dialogue by witnessing to the vitality of the great Christian traditions of asceticism and mysticism." [31]

A Pilgrim Among Pilgrims

John Paul II was an extraordinary pastor. His pastoral heart was rooted in a profound grasp of the mysteries of the Catholic faith and the philosophical issues linked with them. In death, as in life, he continued to reach out to millions and to strengthen their faith. He was tested in the crucible of suffering right from his younger days. Already at the age of 18, he had lost all who were dearest to him: his mother, his beloved elder brother, and his father. During his long years as Pope, suffering continued to keep him company. Is it not that in the crucible of suffering the loving providence of God opened to him the way to the human heart?

What was it about this Pope that could electrify crowds of thousands and tens of thousands of people? His closeness to human existence and his unshakeable faith in the Lord Jesus are the foundations of the splendid anthropology that he proposed. During a papacy of over 26 years, he was able to give witness to his closeness to the Lord Jesus and to the human family. It is worth recalling how the Pontiff synthesised the Christian anthropology. "The revealed truth concerning man

---

[30] *Ibid.*, n.16.

[31] John Paul II, *Apostolic Exhortation, Ecclesia in Asia* (6 November 1999) n. 1-51, in *Insegnamenti di Giovanni Paolo II*, 22/2, Città del Vaticano, Libreria Editrice Vaticana, 2002, n.31.

as 'the image and likeness' of God constitutes the immutable *basis of all Christian anthropology.*"[32] Made in the image and likeness of God, people are called on to live their lives in a manner worthy of this great dignity. John Paul II indeed recognised the holiness of people. He beatified 1,338 and canonised 482 during his Pontificate.

What was the secret of John Paul II's extraordinary charism? His total surrender to the Lord, his complete availability to be lead by the Spirit and his motto *Totus Tuus ego sum* give indications of this secret.

John Paul II was a sign and symbol of the Universality of the Church. By his tremendous openness, he taught people how to unite the members of the human family around life. In embracing a child, he felt the future of the family and he embraced humanity. His contemplation of Christ illumined for him both the splendour and the fragility of the human person. As he journeyed on the roads of this world as Pope for 26 years, he carried the light of Christ. People greeted him with the words, "Holy Father." On the roads of our nations, we recognised him as a father who understood and embraced.

> "How can I not embrace with grateful memory all the bishops of the world whom I have met in "ad limina Apostolorum" visits! How can I not recall so many non-Catholic Christian brothers! And the rabbi of Rome and so many representatives of non-Christian religions! And how many representatives of the world of culture, science, politics, and of the means of social communication!"[33]

---

[32] John Paul II, *Mulieris dignitatem*, 1988, n. 6.

[33] John Paul II, *Last Will and Testament*. Official English Translation of Pope John Paul II Last Will and Testament Vatican, April 7, 2005 (Life SiteNews.com). Following is the text of the spiritual testament of John Paul II, which was released today in an Italian translation of the original Polish. The translation from Italian into English has been done by the Vatican Information Service: *http://www.lifesite.net/ldn/2005/apr/05040703.html* (accessed on 16/4/2005).

A Pilgrim Building Bridges of Friendship and Reconciliation

The Pontificate of John Paul II was marked by quality relationship with believers of other religions. Through his contribution towards other religions, he proposed brilliant and bold steps for the reflection of Christian communities. He was an expert in reconciling peoples and nations, in breaking new ground and in proclaiming the Great Jubilee. A diaconia of reconciliation and journeying together was made possible, thanks to his numerous initiatives. He was the first Pope to visit a synagogue, the memorial at Auschwitz to victims of the Holocaust, and a mosque, when he visited a 1,300-year-old Islamic house of worship in Damascus, Syria.

The paradigmatic metaphor of Assisi inaugurated by John Paul II is a lasting memorial of inter-religious dialogue. October 27 1986, will forever remain a red-letter day in the history of humanity. On that memorable day, for the first time in history, representatives of religions gathered in Assisi to pray together. Assisi, no doubt, is a landmark in the encounter of religions. This encounter assumes a profound meaning when seen in the light of the known or unknown, documented or non-documented, organised or non-organised, daily or occasional encounters that have taken place in multi-religious contexts in history between believers of various religions. Who can ever deny the depth of richness of daily personal encounters and dynamic interaction in most pluralistic societies?

John Paul II, in his apostolic letter *Tertio Millennio Adveniente,* announced "the advent of a new millennium offers a great opportunity for inter-religious dialogue and for meeting with the leaders of the great world religions" (TMA n.53). History is gradually introducing humanity into the naked reality that inter-religious dialogue is at its best when it is beyond minutely calculated and organised activities. In terms of life and death, peoples are capable of passing over doctrinal differences in religions and meet together as brothers and sisters. It is opportune to reflect on religions around one table.

A Pilgrim of Hope in Good Health and in Sickness

The pontificate of John Paul II leaves a prodigious legacy of Magisterium woven out of the fabric of human life in its multifaceted forms and in its various concerns. He courageously proclaimed the Good News of God's love in good health and in sickness. Those who accompanied him during his pontificate were able to grasp the power of Christianity that shines out in the weakness of people. Apostle Paul has expressed it eloquently: "Three times I besought the Lord about this, that it should leave me; but he said to me, 'My grace is sufficient for you, for my power is made perfect in weakness'" (2 Cor 12:8-9).

In a world where efficiency and success are the norm of life, it is rather difficult to go against the current and to witness to the Gospel. John Paul II has left to the human family a lasting testimony of courage and dedication to the end. Familiarity with the Cross of Christ indeed is the secret that keeps the flame of faith alive in the midst of trials and sufferings. "Christians who live by faith habitually make the Cross of Christ their point of reference and norm of living."[34] This in no way is an abstract concept. It is indeed a style of living in which the believer gradually learns through a dialogical relationship with Jesus Christ. The act of embracing the Cross is a consequence of the readiness to serve Him. Here, there is an *in-between* that needs to be considered in the light of the salvific significance of the Cross. For the believer it is that sacred space, that inner sanctuary, the very heart of his or her being loved, accepted and known in its totality only by the Lord. For those around

---

[34] John Paul II, *Master in Faith*, n. 16.

this *in-between* is that something that makes the person so different from every one else. For the Spirit of the Lord, this *in-between* is that horizon of the person's being where one is most open and available to be modelled and re-modelled till the loving designs of God is accomplished in its fullness in and through that person. In a dialogical relationship with the Lord, in complete freedom, the person says his or her amen to the divine plan. In most cases, it is through the weakness of the human person that the power of the Lord is made visible. This in no way wants to lessen the struggle that the person concerned has to go through in order to let the power of the Lord be "made perfect in weakness." Who can erase from our hearts that memorable icon of the *urbi et orbi* of the last Easter Sunday of John Paul II's life?

> None of us can ever forget how in that last Easter Sunday of his life, the Holy Father, marked by suffering, came once more to the window of the Apostolic Palace and one last time gave his blessing 'urbi et orbi.' We can be sure that our beloved Pope is standing today at the window of the Father's house, that he sees us and blesses us. Yes, bless us, Holy Father.[35]

A Pilgrim in Dialogue with the Young Pilgrims

A great wooden cross, a multitude of youth gathered together and an ageing pontiff—do these images communicate to us something about the education of young people today? The purpose of education, as Cardinal Newman defined it, is to "educate the intellect to reason well in all matters, to reach out towards truth, and to grasp it."

Be it be at Buenos Aires (1987), Campostella (1988), Czestochowa (1991) Manila (1995), Paris (1997) or Rome (2000),

---

[35] Joseph Ratzinger, Homily at John Paul II's funeral Mass on April 8, 2005 in St. Peter's Square in *Zenit.org* (accessed on 10/4/2005). [Original text in Italian; translation issued by Holy See] ZE05040802.

these images left a great ray of hope not only in the hearts of the teeming millions of youngsters over the world, but also in that of the large humanity that followed the great World youth days. Is it not still fresh in our minds that evocative image of the great "Gateway" in the field at Tor Vergata in Rome on the evening of the 19 August 2000 at the start of the vigil of the 15th World Youth Day? "Hand in hand with five young people from the five continents, I (John Paul II) crossed the threshold under the gaze of the crucified and risen Christ. In a way it was symbolic: I was entering into the third millennium accompanied by all of you."[36]

"Young people of every continent do not be afraid to be the saints of the new millennium!" John Paul II has been accompanying the youth for the last two decades proposing to them challenging messages and entrusting to them formidable responsibilities. He doesn't seem to minimise the problems that young people are facing today; in fact, he exhorts them to be witnesses in the midst of the concrete realities of day-to-day life and traces out for the young the mission lands where they are called to be witnesses and places the world of the young people as one of the main:

> The same world of young people, dear friends, is a mission land for the Church today. Everyone knows the problems which plague the environment in which young people live: the collapse of values, doubt, consumerism, drugs, crime, eroticism, etc. But at the same time every young person has a great thirst for God, even if at times this thirst is hidden behind an attitude of indifference or even hostility. How many young people, lost and dissatisfied, went to Czestochowa to give a deeper and more decisive meaning to

---

[36] Message of The Holy Father of The Youth of The World on The Occasion of The XVI World Youth Day *http://www.vatican.va/holy father/ john paul ii/messages/youth/documents/hf jp-ii mes 20010215 xvi-world-youth-day en.html* (accessed on 09/01/2002).

their lives! How many came from a distance — not only in a geographical sense — although they were not baptized! I am sure that for many young people the meeting in Czestochowa was a form of pre-evangelization; for others it marked an essential turning-point, an occasion of genuine conversion. [...], because it is young people who 'should become the first apostles of the young, in direct contact with them, exercising the apostolate by themselves among themselves' [...] this is a basic principle of educating in faith. Here, then, is your great task![37]

It is important to mention that the Pope's messages to the young are filled with hope: "There are places and circumstances where you alone can bring the seed of God's Word." He invites the young to an active involvement in the world: "A disciple of Christ is never a passive and indifferent observer of what is taking place. On the contrary, he feels responsible for transforming social, political, economic and cultural reality." The Pope commissions young people of every continent to take up the challenge of becoming saints: "Do not be afraid to be the saints of the new millennium! Be contemplative, love prayer; be coherent with your faith and generous in the service of your brothers and sisters, be active members of the Church and builders of peace."

"To become builders of a civilisation of love and truth" — John Paul II frankly tells the young people that he holds them in his heart:

Yes - as I assured you on that unforgettable World Day celebrated in Paris — the Pope thinks about you and loves you; he reaches out to you daily with affectionate thoughts and

---

[37] Message of The Holy Father Pope John Paul II For The VII World Youth Day *http://www.vatican.va/holy father/john paul ii/messages/youth/ documents/hf jp-ii mes 24111991 vii-world-youth-day en.html* (accessed on 09/01/2002).

accompanies you with prayer; he trusts you and counts on you, on your Christian commitment and on your collaboration in the Gospel cause." [38]

He challenges them to meet Christ in their daily life:

Indeed, I come in spirit to you with this same wish, to meet you in every corner of the earth, wherever you face the intense, daily adventure of life: in your families, where you study or work, in the communities where you gather to hear the word of the Lord and to open your hearts to him in prayer (Message for the XIth World Youth Day).

From an unceasing appeal to open the doors to Christ, his messages to the young takes on the tone of a growing commitment to become personally aware of the Father's infinite love for each of them, to know Jesus, to contemplate him, to be open to learn all things from the Spirit and to bear witness to Jesus in the present world. In fact, he boldly exhorts them: "Being disciples of Christ is not a private matter. On the contrary, the gift of faith must be shared with others." The formidable task John Paul II entrusts to the young is that of fixing their glance at the future:

I am appealing especially to you, young people, to look to the epochal threshold of the Year 2000, remembering that 'the future of the world and the Church belongs to the younger generation, to those who, born in this century, will reach maturity in the next, the first century of the new millennium...If they succeed in following the road which he points out to them, they will have the joy of making their own contribution to his presence in the next century' (*Tertio millennio adveniente,* n. 58). By conforming your daily life to the Gospel of the one Teacher who has 'the words of eternal

---

[38] Message of The Holy Father Pope John Paul II For The XIII World Youth Day 1997 *http://www.vatican.va/holy father/john paul ii/messages/ youth/documents/hf jp-ii mes 09011998 xiii-world-youth-day en.html* (accessed on 09/01/2002).

life', you will be able to become genuine workers for justice, following the commandment which makes love the new 'frontier' of Christian witness. This is the law for transforming the world [cf. *Gaudium et spes,* n. 38] (1995 message).

According to John Paul II, the World Youth Day in Canada was another chance to meet Christ, to bear witness to his presence in today's society and to become builders of the "civilisation of love and truth." The pope wishes the young to be the "saints of the third millennium! Ours is the wonderful and demanding task of becoming its 'reflection'" (No. 54). "Come, and make the great avenues of Toronto resound with the joyful tidings that Christ loves every person and brings to fulfilment every trace of goodness, beauty and truth found in the city of man."[39]

From the Roads of the World in Pilgrimage to St. Peter's, Rome

The purpose of this pilgrimage was clear: to pay homage to the Pope and to express gratitude to him. He taught the world how to follow Jesus in the context of Christianity today. The pilgrimage was carried out in a profound attitude of faith; the fatigue of the journey was not measured.[40] Hours of waiting were interspersed with praise, thanks and invocations! Hymns and prayers were chanted in all languages. It was the hour of a new Pentecost. The universality of the Church offered space

---

[39] Message of the Holy Father to The Youth of The World on The Occasion of The XVII World Youth Day (Toronto 18-28 July 2002). *http:/ /www.vatican.va/holy father/john paul ii/messages/youth/documents/hf jp-ii mes 20010731 xvii-world-youth-day en.html* (accessed on 08/01/2002).

[40] Cf. Davide Rondoni, *Questa fila non era nei conti,* in *Avvenire,* Mercoledì 6 aprile 2005, 1.

to every local culture and to every people and nation. It was in this distinguishing characteristic of the Church that *communitas* was strongly experienced and in almost perfect organisation. Around John Paul II the Pilgrim of peace, the human family was gathered, in a moment of communion and of hope. It seemed as if sorrows and joys embraced each other, proclaiming once again to the world and, in particular, to the believer that death is not the end. "Death is the end of man's earthly pilgrimage, of the time of grace and mercy which God offers him" (CCC 013).

The crowd shouted, "John Paul II." How many times this shout was heard over and over again in the square of St. Peter's? Can the human family forget the charismatic figure of this Pontiff and his ability to speak to each one in an individual way? Yes, John Paul II, it was not difficult to recognise that he was a mystic: a man of deep prayer and contemplation. Who are you searching for?[41] This penetrating question of yours is not only reflected on by people, but millions and millions were convinced of the one he had sought and found—Jesus Christ. This secret gave meaning to the presence of this immense crowd of pilgrims. Their glance fixed on his remains, their tears, their shouts of joy and the kisses they blew towards you become meaningful only when interiorised in the light of contemplation and mysticism. He was a Pilgrim among pilgrims. The immense crowds of pilgrims gathered at St. Peter's Square and around Rome to bid him farewell give testimony of a serene, painful, yet joyful pilgrimage. In John Paul II's numerous pilgrimages and in this final pilgrimage of the world to say goodbye to him, there is great possibility to reflect on pilgrimage as a 'liminoid phenomenon.'

---

[41] Cf. Annalisa Guglielmino, *Sul treno dei pellegrini: "Ci ripeterebbe: chi cercate"? in Avvenire,* Mercoledì 6 aprile 2005, 5.

A Time for Pilgrims to Refresh the Memory of the Heart

In the liminal space of life and death, pilgrimage is a time to refresh the memory of the heart. "Liminality is the mother of invention."[42] John Paul II's pilgrimage to the world made us aware of what a great mystic he was. "Our pilgrimage to Rome dear John Paul II, was the tangible expression of pilgrimage as the mysticism of the crowd." In this immense crowd, people stood as one with individual religious identity. The ties of love and brotherhood bound people together, a force that united them. It was the power of Christ that John Paul II tried to communicate. It is what we have seen, what we have heard and what we cherish in our hearts. There were those who have come to return his visit to them; there were others who were attracted by the power of his words; there were those who were moved by his witness of life: his ability to ask pardon, to forgive and build bridges of reconciliation. There are those who had carved those significant words of his on their hearts: "Help the Pope and all those who want to serve Christ and, with the power of Christ, serve man and the entire humanity! Do not be afraid! Open,[43] rather open wide the doors to Christ!"

> The mystery of the Incarnation therefore reshapes the universal experience of 'sacred space', on the one hand relativizing it, and on the other hand underlining its importance in new terms. The very 'taking of flesh' by the Word (*Jn* 1:14) is in fact a reference to space. In Jesus of Nazareth, God has assumed the features typical of human nature, including a person's belonging to a particular people and a particular land.[44]

[42] Victor Turner, *Symbols and Social Experience in Religious Ritual* in *Studio Missionalia* 23 (1974), 10.

[43] John Paul II, *Omelia di Giovanni Paolo II per l'inizio del Pontificato,* Domenica, 22 ottobre 1978 in *http://www.vatican.va/holy father/john paul ii/speeches/1978/documents/hf jp-ii spe 19781022 inizio-pontificato it.html* (accessed on 8/4/2005).

[44] John Paul II, *Concerning pilgrimage,* n.3.

As the worldwide human family said farewell to John Paul II, that very universal experience of "sacred space" reshaped by the mystery of Incarnation, relativising, and highlighting its significance in new terms was stretched to such an extent by the Spirit of Christ that blows freely to transform street squares into sanctuaries. Couldn't this new Pentecost be read as a tangible expression of the mystery of the Incarnation reshaping the universal experience of "sacred space"?

"Pilgrimages evoke our earthly journey toward heaven and are traditionally very special occasions for renewal in prayer. For pilgrims seeking living water, shrines are special places for living the forms of Christian prayer in Church." **(CCC 2691).**

Turning Street Squares into Sanctuaries

The beautiful metaphor of pilgrimage is the connecting link between members of various religions. Pilgrimage seen from an anthropological and mystical perspective inevitably leads to pilgrimage stations marked for their sacredness. Pilgrimage as mysticism of the crowd calls for turning street squares into sanctuaries, filled with prayer. The street squares were transformed into sanctuaries, making it possible for every one to participate fully in the funeral Eucharist, and to bid farewell to John Paul II. The pilgrimage stations with their sacredness attracted pilgrims to prayer. Pilgrimage is an auspicious journey during which the moral truths of the believing community are communicated in different ways.

Pilgrimage in the liminal space of life and death indeed is an occasion for those who are alive to celebrate the faith that sustained the departed. This is done in the spirit of solidarity and brotherhood. A sea of people, made up of presidents, pilgrims and bishops, said a touching farewell to Pope John Paul II at the funeral Mass at St. Peter's Square. Millions around Rome and countless hundreds of millions worldwide followed the more than two-and-a-half hour Eucharistic celebration through television and radio. After the Mass, bells tolled and twelve pallbearers presented the coffin to the crowd, and then carried it on their shoulders back inside the basilica for burial in the midst the sustained applause of dignitaries from 138 nations and the crowds at the square chanting "santo subito", "sainthood at once." According to the data available from the municipality, 3 million pilgrims travelled to Rome to say goodbye to the Pope. In two thousand years of Christianity, it was the first time Rome received so many pilgrims, as it did for John Paul II's funeral.

An Anticipated Pilgrimage Cologne, August 2005, 20th World Youth Day

Pilgrimage as mysticism of the crowd goes beyond every planned appointment. It is a journey that is undertaken, moved not so much by the logic of time and convenience but by a conviction of heart. It is indeed a pilgrimage prompted by love, affection and esteem and lived in the great spirit of communitas. The passing away of John Paul II and the crowds of young pilgrims who poured into Rome made a number of journalists conclude that: "John Paul II's funeral was a veritable 'World Youth Day', a 'historic event.'"[45]

"The atmosphere one senses here is that of a World Youth Day; I think the Pope anticipated" the next Youth Day scheduled this August in Germany, said Father Josetxo Vera of "Popular Television" of Navarre, Spain. The great pilgrimage of young people to Rome to bid farewell to John Paul II was interspersed by prayer, the sacrament of reconciliation, pilgrimage to St. John Lateran and testimonies, a sign that the young pilgrims were on their way.

---

[45] *Shades of Another World Youth Day* Rome, April 10, 2005 (*Zenit.org*).

'Rise, let us be on our way!' —with these words he roused us from a lethargic faith, from the sleep of the disciples of both yesterday and today. 'Rise, let us be on our way!' he continues to say to us even today.

> Our Pope—and we all know this—never wanted to make his own life secure, to keep it for himself; he wanted to give of himself unreservedly, to the very last moment, for Christ and thus also for us. And thus he came to experience how everything which he had given over into the Lord's hands, came back to him in a new way. His love of words, of poetry, of literature, became an essential part of his pastoral mission and gave new vitality, new urgency, new attractiveness to the preaching of the Gospel, even when it is a sign of contradiction.[46]

Mystics on the Streets of Rome

John Paul II was a mystic who had the courage to challenge others to meditation and contemplation. Often he invited the pilgrims to undertake the interior journey. During his pilgrimage and especially in his contacts with other religions he saw the urgent need for contemplation. Pilgrimage as mysticism of the crowd was an expression of the dynamic dialogue that continued after the Pontiff's death. John Paul II, during his 26 years of papacy, had broken new ground in inter-religious dialogue and had "touched the people of other faiths." James Donahue, the president of the Graduate Theological Union in Berkeley, a consortium of Protestant and Catholic seminaries, called the pope "a moral and spiritual hero for Catholics and non-Catholics alike." "He took the papacy out of the Vatican," said Donahue, a Catholic theologian.[47] Almost

---

[46] Joseph Ratzinger, *Homily at John Paul II's funeral Mass*.

[47] Don Lattin, Peter Fimrite, Chronicle Staff Writers, in *San Francisco Chronicle http://sfgate.com/cgi-bin/article.cgi?file=/c/a/2005/04/02/ MNGB3C2BBC1.DTL* (accessed on 8/5/2005).

like a fraternal exchange, the immense crowd of pilgrims rushed to Rome bringing the world to the Vatican. How many came from a distance—not only in a geographical sense... Reflections on pilgrimage as mysticism of the crowd have to take into account also the "distance" in the psychological, pedagogical and every other possible sense. As family of religions, this task has to be addressed in the spirit of the "Family of Truth." Mysticism, as it is common to all religions, may indicate ways to bridge the distance.

City of Rome — An Open Home for the World

To say thanks to John Paul II the Great Pilgrim, representatives from the five continents travelled to Rome. The city of Rome opened wide its doors to welcome pilgrims of every nation, race and people. Streams of persons gathered at St. Peters Square and on every possible street corner, waiting patiently and silently to say goodbye to the Pontiff. Here we have a powerful testimony to how one can be a connecting link in the liminal space between life and death. The "open margin" is where humanity is. John Paul II "embraced this margin", placing his whole being at the service of humanity. His style of "bridging the margin" so eloquently spoke to the world because the human family experienced that he knew well the human condition and for what human hearts thirst. His diakonia of love in the service of humanity addressed issues that threaten life. He was a messenger of life and of hope.

Mysticism of the Crowd, Communitas and the Family of Truth

With John Paul II on the scene, communitas just sprang up. Crowds gathered around him during his pilgrimages to the world. This spontaneous communitas with all its positive aspects became structured as pilgrims got back to their homes. Even in the midst of strong moments of communitas, the pope was able to lead the pilgrims into deep prayer, silence and contemplation. The commitments he entrusted to the people and the groups present, in most cases, called for community collaboration and personal commitment. Communitas generates enthusiasm and freshness to return to structures with renewed vigour.

Pilgrimage as mysticism of the crowd is a lived expression of communitas in the "Family of Truth." Only members of a family are capable of forgetting all differences and gathering together in moments of profound sorrow and deep loss like the death of a dear one. Who can deny that the funeral of John Paul II offered a tangible opportunity for inter-religious dialogue and for meeting with the leaders of the great religions? The family of religions, fully aware of their doctrinal differences, knew how to unite at St. Peter's Square after the death of John Paul II. It was at the same square that representatives of various religions pledged to unite to face challenges at the conclusion of the World Assembly of Religions (24-29 October 1999). The pope had shared with the participants the interest in dialogue among religions, which is one of the signs of hope.

> I am convinced that the increased interest in dialogue between religions is one of the signs of hope present in the last part of this century (cf. *Tertio Millennio Adveniente*, 46). Yet there is a need to go further. Greater mutual esteem and growing trust must lead to still more effective and coordinated common action on behalf of the human family.[48]

Pilgrimage as Mysticism of Members of Various Religions

Turner has stressed the social splendour of religion. Pilgrimage as mysticism of the crowd, as seen in the liminal space that

---

[48] John Paul II, *Discorso del Santo Padre all'Assemblea Interreligiosa*, Piazza San Pietro, 28 ottobre 1999 in *http://www.vatican.va/holy father/ john paul ii/speeches/1999/october/documents/hf jp-ii spe 281 01999* inter-religious-assembly en.html, n.4 (accessed on 18/4/2005).

followed John Paul II's death until his funeral, provides an opportunity to reflect on the social splendour of religion. This splendour is made visible through the personal and communitarian life of those who believe. The profound experience of holiness according to one's own God leads the believer into the mystical experience.

> Mysticism is the point of convergence between religions precisely in the progressive abandonment of self towards a more profound availability to the free eruption of the mystery. The foundation common to all religions exactly is the dialectic of journey that reveals the twofold truth of man: his nothingness animated and elevated by the exacting and gratifying presence of God.[49]

The attitude that the human person assumes before the eruption of the mystery is of utmost importance. The willingness of the person to make himself or herself available, so that the eruption of the mystery can take place in all its fullness, is a process. The progressive abandonment of self is a conscious and responsible act on the part of the person. This demands giving up one's own cherished ideas, ways of seeing, planning, etc. This means going against the current. Silence, solitude, courage to stand-alone, prayer and contemplation are all necessary to enter into mysticism. The extraordinary development of mass media offers a splendid possibility for a greater visibility[50] of religion in the post-modern society.

---

[49] Michael Fuss, *Unità e pluralismo delle forme dell'esperienza di Dio. Nella prospettiva della fenomenologia delle religioni*, in Associazione Teologica Italiana, Maurizio Aliotta (a cura) *Cristianesimo, religione, religioni. Unità e pluralismo dell'esperienza di Dio alle soglie del terzo millennio*, Milano, San Paolo, 1999, 81.

[50] Cf. Stefano Martelli, *Tra Roma e Gerusalemme. Il dialogo inter-religioso nei mass media in occasione dei pellegrinaggi di Giovanni Paolo II nell'Anno giubilare*, in Roberto De Vita e Fabio Berti (a cura di), *La Religione nella Società dell'incertezza per una convivenza solidale in una società multireligiosa*, Milano, FrancoAngeli, 2001, 217-241.

A Pope who Linked Mysticism and the Media

John Paul II, the great communicator of God's love to the human family, found in the media of communications a powerful means to proclaim his message. The world of communications accompanied him in his apostolic pilgrimages.

The entire world witnessed how eloquently the media world covered the days of his grave illness and the liminal period that followed his death to his burial (1-8 April). With a marked sense of sacredness, mass media gathered and communicated to the entire human family the sentiments of the countless number of pilgrims.[51] The mysticism of the crowd interrupted by sobs and tears, by claps and shouts moved even the media world.

> The special thing about this pope, this media genius, is that he managed to create a connection between mysticism and the media, between a spiritual approach to life and the media's social packaging and globalization of this phenomenon. This is something new, even in the age of television.[52]

During his Pontificate, John Paul II saw the urgency for New Evangelisation.Is it not that the media of communications[53] offered a sumptuous banquet to the world through the quantity and quality of programmes transmitted on and for John Paul

---

[51] Cf. *"Ecco perché siamo venuti da lui"* in *Avvenire* mercoledì 6 aprile 2005, 4.

[52] German philosopher and Protestant Rüdiger Safranski, in *Der Spiegel. Safranski* April 11, 2005. Quote taken from Understanding the Spirit of John Paul II, Observers try to assess His Inner Life, in (*Zenit.org*). - Rome, April 16, 2005.

[53] Cf. Live transmission of the events, *http://www.vatican.va/news services/television/index.htm*

II? Besides the TV programmes, there is need to remember the International Press.[54]

Cardinal Cormac Murphy-O'Connor described the Holy Father as a "man of deep prayer" who "had a conviction of God's providence running through his life."[55]

The catechesis of the silent audience of Wednesday, 6 April 2005 is a perfect initiation into the liminal period of dialogical immortality. It is an explosion of the faith of the people in the Resurrection of Jesus Christ. It is the people who now almost hand over to John Paul II what they have heard from him and cherished in their hearts.

> Liminality is applicable to all phases of cultural changes precisely because it expresses the 'passing' character of subjective experience in which the preceding relations between idea and subject are put to free disposition, in order to give place a new creativity.[56]

Conclusion

John Paul II, Pilgrim among pilgrims, communicated the good News that Jesus Christ is the way, the truth and the life, with an attentive anthropological reading of the human person and in dialogue with the history of Christianity. He made the world aware that there is a possibility of engaging in a dialogue with faith in respectful listening to the form of religious experience and in prayerful listening of revelation. This was how he stressed that the anthropological is a constant point of reference for theological reflections.

---

[54] Cf. *Il grande Pontificato nella rassegna della stampa internazionale* in L'Osservatore Romano, Giovedì 7 aprile 2005, 7.

[55] Cardinal Cormac Murphy-O'Connor, in *London Telegraph*, April 3, 2005. Quote taken from Understanding the Spirit of John Paul II, Observers try to assess His Inner Life, in (*Zenit.org*). - Rome, April 16, 2005.

[56] Michael FUSS, *Unità e pluralismo*, 65.

The Pope has constantly reminded the human family that the human person is the masterpiece of God and that one realises one's own vocation only in the face of Jesus Christ, the only Son of the Father. To be the image and likeness of God is a constant invitation to plunge into the mystery of the Trinity revealed definitely in Jesus. Here is the real significance of what it means to remember the roots of Christianity. More than being just a mere remembrance, the Christian roots spur on the Christian to try to reach the stature of Christ: to keep Him as the norm of individual existence. Undoubtedly, this is the fruit of intimacy with Him, a dialogical relationship, a living in Jesus, by interiorising His message and making one's own His style of governing as service.

Prophetic, mystical and contemplative instances are always present in religions and wait for an appropriate moment for their development. At the death of John Paul II, pilgrimage exploded as the mysticism of the crowd. Death is a reality that permits a genuine encounter between members of various religions. Where else can we look for the common basis for the experience of God if not in the maximum transparency of the human person? It may be recognised by different names, but all refer to the manifestation of the sacred. How is the genuine encounter among religions built if not in total availability on the part of the person for the free eruption of the Sacred?

John Paul II was truly a pilgrim in dialogue with the young and their educators.

CHAPTER TWO

John Paul II: A Pontiff in Dialogue with the Young and their Educators

Educators Committed to Proclaim, Defend and Spread the Truth

Right from the very beginning of his pontificate, John Paul II has spoken forcefully on education and faith education. Numerous are his interventions on schools both catholic and state, as instrument of cultural formation, for the development of the person, for the search for truth. The occasions for these interventions are meetings with pilgrims or Italian scholastic organisations.[1] To get an overview of the pope's messages on education, we need to look at his teachings. Here we are reminded of the words of Patrick J. in his article "Rules of Thumb for Reading Church Documents." One such rule is: Learn to "see the forest for the trees." According to this author:

---

[1] Ubaldo Gianetto, *Aspetti E Problemi dell'Educazione Cristiana in Atto*, offers quite a detailed information on Christian Education in John Paul II covering the period up to 1989. Cf. *L'Educazione Cristiana negli insegnamenti degli ultimi Pontefici da Pio XI a Giovanni Paolo II*, Norberto Galli (a cura), Milano, 1992, Vita E Pensiero, 95-104.

> Some Church documents are part of a composite whole, a developing tradition. In other words, they compose part of the 'big picture'. That is, when a document seems to speak to a specific time or issue, it should not be seen as trapped in that time or by that issue. Instead, consider the document as but one more thread woven into a living tapestry, say, the creation of God's kingdom on earth or the eschatological culmination of humanity.[2]

A quick glance at the Apostolic Letter *Novo Millennio Ineunte* will offer us the new horizon in which we need to collocate our efforts towards education. It is the profound longing that young people have for genuine values:

> Sometimes when we look at the young, with the problems and weaknesses that characterise them in contemporary society, we tend to be pessimistic. The Jubilee of Young People however changed that, telling us that young people, whatever their possible ambiguities, have a profound longing for those genuine values which find their fullness in Christ" (NMI n°9).

And in n° 55, speaking of dialogue and mission, John Paul II reaffirms:

> In the years of preparation for the Great Jubilee, the Church has sought to build, not least through a series of highly symbolic meetings, *a relationship of openness and dialogue with the followers of other religions*. This dialogue must continue. In the climate of increased cultural and religious pluralism which is expected to mark the society of the new millennium, it is obvious that this dialogue will be especially important in establishing a sure basis for peace and warding off the dread spectre of those wars of religion which have so often bloodied human history. The name of the one God must become increasingly what it is: *a name of peace and a summons to peace.*

---

[2] Patrick J Hayes, *Rules of Thumb for Reading Church Documents, in The Living Light,* Spring 2001, 12.

Keeping in mind the climate of growing cultural and religious pluralism, which is already present in the modern world, we would like to highlight a few salient points to understand the challenges that the Pope offers to educators.

Undoubtedly, we can say that the field on which the Holy Father focuses his attention is that of faith and culture, of cultural progress and of the mission of Universities. He entrusted to teachers and students of the ecclesiastical universities as their priority task "to know and to make known the true image of God."[3]

In his homily for the Jubilee of University Professors on 10 September 2000, John Paul II reminded them that:

> Every day you are committed to proclaiming, defending and spreading the truth. Often this involves truths concerning the most diverse aspects of the cosmos and of history. The subject material will not always touch directly on the problem of the ultimate meaning of life and the relationship with God, as the areas of philosophy and theology. However, this problem abides as the larger context of every thought. Even in research on areas of life which seem quite far from faith there is a hidden desire for truth and meaning which goes beyond the particular and the contingent.[4]

What is most striking is his courage to proclaim that "there is no contradiction, but rather a logical connection, between freedom of research and recognition of truth [...] A culture

---

[3] John Paul II, Homily, Opening of the academic year of Ecclesiastical universities, Friday 20 October 2000,_*http://www.vatican.va/holy father/ john paul ii/homilies/2000/documents/hf jp-ii hom 20001020 eccles-univers en.html* (accessed on 03/04/2011).

[4] John Paul II, Homily, Jubilee of University professors, Sunday 10 September 2000. *http://www.vatican.va/holy father/john paul ii/homilies/2000/ documents/hf jp-ii hom 20000910 jubi-univ-teachers en.html* (accessed on 06/04/2011).

without truth does not safeguard freedom but puts it at risk. I strongly encourage all of you, men and women of the University, to spare no effort in rebuilding that aspect of learning which is open to Truth and the Absolute."[5]

In his address to the administration, faculty, students and staff of the Pontifical Gregorian University on Friday, 6 April 2001, John Paul II once again highlighted the importance of inter-religious dialogue:

> In today's context of a globalized world, where the co-existence of people of different faiths and cultures is more marked and frequent, interreligious dialogue acquires considerable importance, because 'the name of the one God', as I wrote in the Apostolic Letter *Novo millennio ineunte,* 'must become increasingly what it is: a name of peace and a summons to peace' (n. 55). [6]

It is to that unforgettable meeting of Assisi in 1986 that he returns to stress the common origin and common destiny of humanity:

> Let me repeat here what I said at the end of that day of fasting and prayer:

> The very fact that we have come to Assisi from various parts of the world is in itself a sign of this common path which humanity is called to tread. Either we learn to walk together in peace and harmony, or we drift apart and ruin ourselves and others. We hope that this pilgrimage to Assisi has taught us anew to be aware of the common origin and common destiny of humanity. Let us see in it an anticipation of what God would like the developing history of humanity to be: a

---

[5] *http://www.vatican.va/holy father/john paul ii/speeches/2000/jul-sep/ documents/hf jp ii spe 20000909 jubilteachers en.html* (accessed on 03/04/ 2011).

[6] *http://www.vatican.va/holy father/john paul ii/speeches/2001/documents/ hf jp-ii spe 20010406 univ-gregoriana en.html* (accessed on 04/04/2011).

> fraternal journey in which we accompany one another toward the transcendent goal which he sets for us (*Address at the Conclusion of the World Day of Prayer for Peace*, Assisi, 27 October 1986, 5).

John Paul II, in his letter to the families,[7] dated 2 February 1994, in n°16, gives a long description of education. In his view:

> Education then is before all else *a reciprocal 'offering' on the part of both parents:* together they communicate their own mature humanity to the newborn child, who gives them in turn the newness and freshness of the humanity which it has brought into the world. He affirms forcefully that parents are *'educators because they are parents'*.

He goes on to stress that parents share their educational mission with other individuals or institutions and exhorts that the mission of education must always be carried out in accordance with a proper application of the "principle of subsidiarity."

John Paul II evidenced the urgent need for Christian Education today in the letter *Juvenum Patris* (n°s 14-19). Here is a very brief mention of the main points, a meditative reading of the entire comment is necessary to collocate these points in the right context.[8]

- Pastoral option for the young. "Let us go to the young: that is the first and fundamental need in the field of education" (n° 14)—Don Bosco's fundamental apostolic option for the poor youth, to those of the lower classes, those most at risk.

- Gospel and education as task (n°15)

- A pedagogy of sanctity as final goal (n°16)

---

[7] *http://www.vatican.va/holy father/john paul ii/letters/documents/hf jp-ii let 02021994 families en.html* (accessed on 03/04/2011).

[8] Cf. Cesare Bissoli, *Il Papa interpreta il sistema educativo di don Bosco*, Leumann (Torino), Elledici, 2000, 128-134.

- To educate and to do so with competence (n°17)

- Some places as privileged educative environment for the young (n° 18)

- Some typical educative moments as style (n°19)

Educators have an un-substitutable role to play in the education of the young, to help them to become what they should be. The words of John Paul II are a challenge not only to the young, but also to their educators: "From Rome, from the City of Peter and Paul, the Pope follows you with affection and, paraphrasing Saint Catherine of Siena's words, reminds you: 'If you are what you should be, you will set the whole world ablaze!'" (cf. *Letter* 368).[9]

In a world characterised by religious pluralism, how can we educate the young to become what they should be?

Religious Pluralism and Education

Today, religious pluralism is one of the main challenges that educators are called to address. What seemed to be the supporting pillars of cultures, societies and people are questioned nowadays. Alternative systems of thought are proposed in subtle and well-decorated packets. In the name of peace and justice and freedom, even terrorism proposes its own message. How can we translate into pastoral action the great principles of dialogue among believers of other religions and related themes? How can we train educators and youngsters to put into effect the paradigm of Assisi?

The concept of pluralism is characterised by the idea of "plurality", of "multiplicity." Pluralism acquires specific

---

[9] Closing of World Youth Day, *Homily Of The Holy Father John Paul II*, Tor Vergata, Sunday 20 August 2000, *http://www.vatican.va/holy father/ john paul ii/homilies/2000/documents/hf jpii hom 20000820 gmg en.html* (accessed on 09/04/2011).

significance according to the field in which it is used. For example, in Philosophy, pluralism refers to a theory or system of thought that recognises more than one ultimate principle. The knowable world, as it is evident, is made up of a plurality of interesting things.

To a great extent, we can say that pluralism is the "fruit of modernity."[10] Today there is awareness of the need for a positive evaluation of the phenomenon of pluralism. It is definitely an expression of the recognition of personal rights and, of course, contributes to the promotion of justice and peace. Pluralism brings possibilities and risks to the field of education.

Alberich lays emphasis on the following points: in a pluralistic society, educative work can receive not few stimulations and profit from possibilities unknown in the past: promotion of the personality open to dialogue and respect of difference; wider horizons of cultural enrichment; overcoming of prejudices and closed-up attitudes, new possibilities of maturation in the critical sense.

The existence of negative consequences of pluralism cannot be overlooked. In the field of education of the young, Alberich points out that: the process of socialisation is strongly modified and shaken as much as the multiplicity exasperated and contradictory of cultural messages is often translated in the impossibility of a coherent personal integration, in the lack of values and therefore in the incapacity of maturation of one's identity.

---

[10] Emilio Alberich, *Pluralism* in *Dizionario di Scienze dell'Educazione* (a cura di Josè Manuel Prellezo [coord]Carlo Nanni, Guglielmo Malizia), Torino, Elle Di Ci, 1997, 834.

A Close Look at Religious Pluralism

In every sphere of nature, plurality is a natural phenomenon. Diversity adds to the richness of life. Beauty can be found only in diversity. In such a context, the plurality of religions becomes a fascinating challenge; "what is required of us is to face the fact of plurality of religions with a sense of admiration and respect for diversity, and sincere attempt to establish a harmonious human society. This is what we call 'religious pluralism' in the positive sense."[11]

The Church has made her own journey in respecting other religions; she considers other religions as humble, sincere and human search for God. Today, sincere efforts are made by the Church to help her sons and daughters enter the art of discovering the "seeds of the Word" present in these religions. In a pluralistic religious set-up, attention needs to be focused on educating youth to appreciate their own religion and that of others. Shocklay also attaches significance to pluralism:

> Pluralism is a method of analysis to aid in critical educating, focusing and objectifying. Absolutes, universals and exclusive revelations are valid in themselves and they are valid for those who believe in them. They are elements of the larger truth or the whole of truth or the whole of truth which by definition is unknowable by a single individual. The pluralist would further suggest that there are elements of the truth in every statement of it. The most productive way to arrive at the truth is to intercommunicate the truth that one holds with truths that others hold. The result of such dialogue could be an enlargement of the truth held by each engaged in such a dialogue.[12]

---

[11] Statement of the (International) Seminar on 'Challenges to Religious Pluralism' *in Challenges to religious pluralism*, A. Pushparajan (Ed), The commission for dialogue, Madurai, 1994, 20.

[12] Grants Shockley, *Religious pluralism and religious education a black protestant perspective* in *Religious pluralism and religious education*, 141.

Renewed Focus on Education

Children are our most valuable natural resource (Herbert Hoover 1874-1964 31st U.S. President). Today, many persons, families and institutions are focusing their reflections on education. John Paul II stresses the need to "promote a spirituality of communion,[13] making it the guiding principle of education" (NMI n.43). The Dalai Lama and a team of experts highlighted the universal responsibility of education[14] to bring out humanitarian change in society. The participants of November 12 Symposium in New York[15] affirmed that "Interfaith Conversation, Education (is) Crucial to 'Dialogue Among Civilizations." There are others who have suggested indicators for an educative proposal for the future.

The marvelous task of education in a pluralistic religious context throws open splendid opportunities for educators. It challenges them to initiate the youngsters to behold the splendour and beauty of each religion. Certainly, the task is both committing and at the same time rewarding. Religious pluralism challenges educators to go beyond just mere knowledge of religions, to grasp even the nuance of each religion to build up a "Family of Truth." This book aims at helping people to begin to think together, and so we propose a practical part on how to put into practice the paradigm of

---

[13] John Paul II, *Novo Millennio Ineunte* [NMI] (6 January 2001).

[14] A book on *"Dialogues on Universal Responsibility and Education"* was announced. The book is supposed to be the fruit of two workshops held in New Delhi between the Dalai Lama and a group of Indian scholars, philosophers, teachers and social reformers. Based on the concept of universal responsibility, the participants discussed ways to bring about humanitarian change in society, focusing on education to effect positive change.

[15] *http://www.wcrp.org/RforP/SYMPOSIUM MAIN.html* (accessed on 03/03/2001).

Assisi. This is just an expression of our conviction that educators are in the best position to translate into pastoral action the great paradigm of Assisi.

A New Group of Educators

The ever-growing demand for a religiosity that can respond to the need of men and women today calls for a new group of educators who can network to facilitate dynamic interaction between the rich cultural patrimony and the deep-rooted religious dimension present and active in every single person. Today, we live in the epoch of pluralism, as people around the globe are becoming ever more conscious of their particular story and are making mindful efforts to allow it to grow, develop and remain a living part of history. "Religious pluralism has become an intellectual and spiritual fact for contemporary life."[16]

A Precious Methodology of Inter-religious Dialogue

Vatican II urged the Catholics to take a wider and responsible look at the world and to pay particular attention to the people of other religions. Decrees of Vatican II: "Declaration on the Church's relation to Non-Christian Religions *Nostra aetate*" is still considered as the "Magna Carta" of inter-religious dialogue for our times.

Declaration on religious freedom *Dignitatis humanae* offered a strong impulse to the Church to enter into a dialogue with members of other religions. Today, the Church in her mission of accompanying persons on their journey to the fullness of life is attentive to establish contact, enter into dialogue and join hands in co-operation with the followers of other religions.

---

[16] Donald Dawe., *'Religious Pluralism and the Church'*, in *Journal of Ecumenical Studies* 18 (Fall, 1981), 604.

Thanks to the Church's openness to believers of other religions, she has developed a pedagogy of dialogue and in *Nostra aetate* offered a precious methodology of inter-religious dialogue. First of all, this methodology invites the faithful to make a careful and deeper study of other religions taking into consideration doctrinal contents and the history of religions.

> The Church examines with greater care the relation which she has to non-Christian religions…she reflects at the outset on what men have in common and what tends to promote fellowship among them (n.1).[17]

The Church is always concerned about the human person and it is amazing to see that she reflects at the start on what people have in common and what tends to promote fellowship among them. The Church has a positive evaluation of other religions.

> The Catholic Church rejects nothing of what is true and holy in these religions. She has a high regard for the manner of life and conduct, the precepts and doctrines which, although differing in many ways from her own teaching, nevertheless often reflect a ray of that truth which enlightens all men (n.2).

The Church's high regard for believers of other religions is accompanied by an equally firm exposition of the ecclesial faith, which is carried out taking into consideration the religious context. Today, she carries out her mission in an attitude that is indisputably contextual and dialogical.

> Yet she proclaims and is in duty bound to proclaim without fail, Christ who is the way, the truth and the life (Jn 1, 6). In him, in whom God reconciled all things to himself (2 Cor 5, 18-19), men find the fullness of their religious life (n. 2).

---

[17] Vatican Council II: *'Declaration on the Church's relation to Non-Christian Religions Nostra aetate'* (October 28, 1965).

Respect for the Freedom and Dignity of Every Person

Dignitatis humanae spells out in clear terms how the Church respects the freedom and dignity of every human person and promotes dialogue: "dialogue of truth." In *Dignitatis humanae* n. 2, important stress is placed on the dynamic aspect of freedom: freedom to seek the truth and to adhere to it; and in n. 3, the manner in which the search for truth needs to be carried out.

> It is in accordance with their dignity as persons, that is, beings endowed with reason and free will and therefore privileged to bear personal responsibility that all men should be at once impelled by nature and also bound by a moral obligation to seek the truth, especially religious truth. They are also bound to adhere to the truth, once it is known, and to order their whole lives in accord with the demands of truth (n.2).[18]

There is a style of carrying out the search for truth. "The search for truth, however, must be carried out in a manner that is appropriate to the dignity of the human person and his social nature, namely by free enquiry with the help of teaching or instruction, communication and dialogue (n.3).

"Freedom attains its full development only by accepting the truth"[19] (CA n. 46).

A Transforming Experience to Narrate

Educators can train their young students to be narrators of their religious experience. At the heart of religion and at the heart of every culture, there is a profound transforming experience. Educating community is a "Family of Truth" on its ongoing journey to discover together the "rays of truth

---

[18] Vatican Council II, *Declaration on religious freedom Dignitatis humanae* (7 December 1965).

[19] John Paul II, Encyclical Letter *Centesimus Annus* (1 May 1991).

present in the religions." Touched by the transforming experience, believers of today, as those of yesterday, have to narrate. The emblematic words of Peter and John, "For we cannot but speak of what we have seen and heard" (Acts 4:20), lead us straight into the heart of narration. Filled with the Holy Spirit, they were narrating their strong experience of Jesus (Cf. Acts 4:1-20).

In each religious tradition, there is someone who dared to believe and found courage and time to narrate his transforming experience. And there were others who listened and got involved in those transforming experiences, thus contributing to the birth of a community of believers. The narrative dynamic keeps the narrator in constant touch with the transforming experience and with the community.

The symbolic words of the two disciples of Emmaus, "Did not our hearts burn within us while he (Jesus) talked to us on the road, while he opened to us the scriptures?" (Luke 24:32), are so often also on the lips of so many believers of today. By retelling the myths, the narrative dimension is kept alive in the believing communities.

The Content of Religious Narration

Everything that has become part of the believer's being, thanks to his or her contact with the divine, is the content of religious narration. The first letter of John eloquently speaks of it:

> That which was from the beginning, which we have heard, which we have seen with our eyes, which we have looked upon and touched with our hands, concerning the word of life—the life was made manifest, and we saw it, and testify to it, and proclaim to you the eternal life which was with the Father and was made manifest to us—that which we have seen and heard we proclaim also to you, so that you may have fellowship with us; and our fellowship is with the Father and with his Son Jesus Christ. And we are writing this that our joy may be complete (1 John 1:1-4).

Believers and communities are born because of narration. In every religion, we can encounter believers who are narrators of their faith-experience and builders of communities. Every conscious and united effort to join hands to relive the supreme values in which each believer believes produces abundance of fruits. And when this is coupled with a firm desire to bear witness to these values in daily life, yes, then there will be true inter-religious dialogue. The service of truth is one of the services that John Paul II proposed to the Church. In his encyclical letter *Fides et Ratio,*[20] he emphasised *Diakonia of the truth* (n° 2) as a specific responsibility that the Church is called to place at the service of humanity. "It is her duty to serve humanity in different ways, but one way in particular imposes a responsibility of a quite special kind: the *diakonia of the truth*" FR 2. Both educators and the youngsters can commit themselves to this task.

Forming Ambassadors of the Diakonia of the Truth

Only through education, we can help our youngsters to understand the *diakonia of the truth* that the Church is asked to render to humanity.

When educators and young people are motivated by the freedom of the human person and the *diakonia of the truth,* they are able to address the challenges that education is called to face today. They are the reality of cultural and religious pluralism, fragmentation of society, lack of values, the reductive concept of the person, etc. Only through a unified educative action, we can discover the common elements of truth. Educators can enthusiastically involve themselves in the service of discovering, unifying, contemplating and proposing the truth to the educating community. The educating community has to allow itself to be guided by the force of the *diakonia of*

---

[20] John Paul II, *Fides et Ratio* (14 September 1998).

the truth in order to face the challenges mentioned above. Education is an intentional call to focus on persons and ideas. Persons are capable of interiorising ideas and putting them into action. Only in this way, a society can produce change and bring about transformation. In the educative process and more precisely in the inter-cultural and multi-religious contexts, search for truth can become an enthralling adventure that strengthens personal and communitarian identities.

To Reinforce One's Religious Identity

Religious identity is necessary for entering into a meaningful dialogue with believers of other religions. How can one's religious identity be strengthened? Identity is a very complex concept with various connotations. "Identity" is the central theme of Erikson's writings. It is identity that received worldwide attention especially in the various stages of development. In his book, *Identity and the Life Cycle*, Erikson, highlights that with a conscious sense of individual identity, an unknown search for a continuity of personal character, a basis for the silent doings of ego synthesis and sustenance of inner solidarity with a group's ideals, the term "identity" assumes various shades and meanings.[21]

The formation of identity is a dynamic ongoing process, under the influence of change and development. It is always in a state of being and becoming. For Erikson, no true intimacy is possible, unless and until the individual has first acquired a "reasonable sense of identity." The person who is not sure of his own identity frequently "shies away from interpersonal intimacy, but the surer he becomes of himself, the more he seeks it in the form of friendship, combat, leadership, love and

---

[21] Cf. Erik Erikson, *Identity and the Life Cycle*, New York, Norton, 1959, 109.

inspiration."[22] Intimacy, in this sense, is seen in its open, wider and more universal perspective and not as often in the general sense it is wrongly interpreted, understood and reduced to just sexual intimacy. When a person is able, with the help of others, to achieve an individual identity in shared intimacy, without losing his or her actual identity, then growth takes place and gradually the person learns to give without losing himself or herself. For Erikson, it is at this stage that the individual begins to accept and interiorise the ethical sense, which is a hallmark of the adult moral and faith development. Identity means to become aware of who we are and to feel secure in that discovery.

Religious identity means to become aware of who we are and what our relationship with the divine is. It means to ask ourselves what is at the heart of our belief system. The question is, to whom are we entrusting our lives? In other words, it means to have the courage to stand for what we believe and to profess it through words, express it in action and celebrate it with symbols. Perhaps Shakespeare says it best of all: "There is a divinity that shapes our ends, rough hew them though we may." This means to know the story of our religion and what riches of religious traditions do we have to contribute to the building up of the human family. This means "always to be prepared to make a defense to anyone who calls you to account for the hope that is in you, yet do it with gentleness and reverence" (1Pt 3, 15). Developing self-identity requires constant reflection on one's life, convictions, hopes, dreams and visions. It is an ongoing task. Knowing one's religious identity puts the person in contact with history made up of the past, the present and the future and offers wisdom to know how to act in the present. Religious identity bestows on the person the sense of belonging to a group. Individual identity is strengthened by group identity.

---

[22] *Ibid., Identity and the Life Cycle*, 101.

Our theme, religious identity and religious pluralism, makes us to probe further, like the ancient Greeks, who, spurred on by the marvel and beauty of things, used to ask the why of things and explored beyond. Educators should explore deep to understand the basic principles that need to be kept in mind in building up religious identity in a religiously pluralistic context. A line from a poem written by Alexander Pope may throw some light:

A little knowledge is a dangerous thing,

Drink deep or taste not the Pierian Spring.

The natural spring waters of Pieria, a town in Thessaly, resided by the Muses, were thought to bestow special gifts of knowledge on the one who drank thereof. Little knowledge on the religion of others is a dangerous thing. We need to drink deep. Strengthening religious identity in a religiously pluralistic context means learning to discover stories of other peoples, to cherish their differences and contributions. It is important to become aware of their needs and, above all, to foster openness and dialogue. In the field of education, learning to appreciate convictions and practices of others requires moving beyond "book learning" to "direct contact" in day-to-day life situations. We need to experience their tradition, their way of looking at reality and their style of celebrating important events of life. Above all, we need to speak the truth in love.

Speaking the Truth in Love

I was deeply struck by the words of a preacher who once said, "The truth will make you free but first it makes you miserable." In fact, learning to speak the truth in love is an art to be appropriated. In a religiously pluralistic context and in the field of education, to speak the truth in love calls for a committed and deliberate journey into other religions.

"Truth" is at the centre of religious faith, because religion is concerned with the ultimate reality. The vision of the ultimate reality upon which our faith is based provides us with a "specific worldview" that serves to guide us towards a particular lifestyle in the direction of the ultimate reality. The fundamental question in religious education is, what are the "truths" to be discovered and how can they be communicated?

Apostle Paul, in his letter to the Philippians, proposes a powerful methodology: "Whatever is true, whatever is honourable, whatever is just, whatever is pure, whatever is lovely, whatever is gracious, if there is any excellence, if there is anything worthy of praise, think about these things" (Phil 4, 8). The search for truth and goodness can open vast horizons and take us everywhere, even to the persons and philosophies that appear to be in discord with our own.

The courage to state our differences and the readiness to accept the consequences may ask us to become a bit "miserable." This is what we mean when we say we need special courage to "speak the truth in love." Intellectual honesty plays a significant role in the search for truth. Honesty coupled with genuine humility opens the road to repentance. In different parts of the world and very often in profound silence, efforts are made to discover the truth and to make it known. "Dabru Emet" is just one example.

"Dabru Emet" (We proclaim the truth) is a Jewish statement[23] dealing with Jewish-Christian relations. It offers "eight brief statements about how Jews and Christians may

---

[23] This statement was issued by the (Baltimore) Institute of Christian Studies, and the National Jewish Scholars Project (released on September 7, 2000). The declaration was "composed by four distinguished academicians" and signed by over 170 rabbis and Jewish scholars from the U.S., Canada, UK and Israel. *http://www.icjs.org/what/njsp/dabruemet.html* (accessed on 31/05/2001).

relate to each other." The title was taken from Zechariah 8:16 and means "speak the truth." This statement is considered to be a "landmark for new and searching conversation between Christians and Jews" and is definitely "an unprecedented shift in Jewish and Christian relations."

Religious pluralism challenges educators and students to cultivate a highly refined attitude of candidness towards other faiths. Only through education people can learn to cross over presuppositions and prejudices to journey deep into the truth that each believer treasures. Through education, we discover that differences of belief call not only for peaceful co-existence, but also for a real search for the truth that each religion expresses. Religious education in a pluralistic society has to go much beyond the simple search for commonness. It demands a constant process of discernment to arrive at the truth.

Conclusion

Prof. Fuss maintains that gathering the "rays of truth" (*Nostra aetate* n.2) means "building up a family of truth."[24] Educational institutions can become honoured places where, accompanied by the wisdom and eloquence of professors and sustained by a sincere committed search for truth, students and the entire educating community work consciously and constantly to collaborate towards the building up of the "family of truth." In this way, the educating community can become a community that is capable of feeling for and with other religions. Learning to speak the truth in love will offer educators the courage to be critical and to denounce when truth is at stake. Pope John Paul II's "Prayer for Peace" encounter in Assisi was indeed a landmark in inter-religious relations.

---

[24] Michael FUSS, *Maria vincolo dell'unità nell'ecumenismo tra le religioni e di fronte ai nuovi movimenti*, in: *Sette e Religioni* 3 (1993) 117.

CHAPTER THREE

The Paradigm of Assisi

John Paul II and Inter-religious Dialogue

The Church's journey towards inter-religious dialogue took a definitive turn during the Pontificate of John Paul II. Ever since that unique encounter of Assisi on 27 October 1986 with the leaders of other religions to pray for peace in the World, the Pope encouraged inter-religious dialogues and gave personal witness through his encounters with leaders of other religions and with his good will to enter into a dialogue with them.

In his Encyclical letter, *Redemptoris Missio*, the pope affirmed that "Interreligious dialogue is a part of the Church's evangelising mission. *Understood as a method and means of mutual knowledge and enrichment*, dialogue is not in opposition to the mission ad gentes; indeed, it has special links with that mission and is one of its expressions" (n. 55).[1]

John Paul II in his Apostolic letter, *Tertio Millennio Adveniente*, announced that "the advent of a new millennium offers a great opportunity for interreligious dialogue and

---

[1] John Paul II, *Encyclical letter Redemptoris Missio* [RM] (7 December 1990).

for meeting with the leaders of the great world religions" (n. 53).[2]

The World Assembly of Religions, held at Vatican City from 24-29 October 1999, was yet another significant event. Francis Cardinal Arinze titled his opening address to the World Assembly of Religions as "World Religions: Join Hands to Face Challenges."[3]

In the Post-Synodal Apostolic Exhortation, *Ecclesia in Asia*, John Paul II emphasised that "ecumenical dialogue and interreligious dialogue constitute a veritable vocation for the Church."[4] "To guide those engaged in the process, the Synod suggested that a directory on inter-religious dialogue be drawn up."[5] To put it in John Paul II's words, "it is therefore important for the Church in Asia to provide suitable models of interreligious dialogue, evangelisation in dialogue and dialogue for evangelisation and suitable training for those involved." The theme "interfaith dialogue" scored 43 out of the 191 interventions in the Synod for Asia.

On 3rd February, to the representatives of the cultural world and of other religions in Calcutta, India, John Paul II said: "Joined in a new solidarity the intellectuals must respond to the challenges of our times."[6] And on 10th February, during

---

[2] *Ibid., Apostolic Letter Tertio Millennio Adveniente (10 November 1994)* n° 53.

[3] Francis Arinze, *World Religions: Join Hands To Face Challenges!* (Opening address to World Assembly of Religions, Vatican City, 25th October 1999), 1-5.

[4] John Paul II, Apostolic Exhortation, *Ecclesia in Asia*, Vatican City, Editrice Vaticana (6 November 1999) n° 29.

[5] John Paul II, Apostolic Exhortation, *Ecclesia in Asia*, 94.

[6] L'Osservatore Romano, Domenica 2 febbraio 1986, XIII.

the homily at mass at the Pontifical Atenaeum of Pune, the Pope forcefully affirmed that "truth united with love is the only force that can radically transform the world."[7]

Assisi an Ever-living Icon of Inter-religious Dialogue

The paradigmatic metaphor of Assisi is John Paul II's unique gift to the World. It is an ever-living icon and a lasting memorial of inter-religious dialogue. October 27, 1986 (Assisi-1), will forever remain as an unforgettable day in the history of humankind. On that memorable day, for the first time in history, representatives of religions gathered in Assisi to pray together. By inviting the leaders of other religions to Assisi, John Paul II "acknowledged the legitimacy of other religions that they can mediate divine-human relationship in prayer which is therefore effective."[8] John Paul II was indeed a champion of friendship and dialogue.[9]

Assisi-One, is certainly a landmark in the encounter of religions. To grasp the significance of this historical event, it should never be viewed as an isolated event. It has to be placed right in the midst of the many dynamic encounters that are taking place day after day in various pluri-religious communities. The unforgettable encounter of Assisi assumes a profound meaning when seen in the light of many known and unknown, documented and non-documented, planned and non-planned, premeditated and occasional daily

---

[7] *Ibid.,* XXXIII.

[8] Michael Amaladoss, *Identity and harmony challenges to mission in South Asia* (Conference, Sedos Missionary Congress, 3-8 April 2000, Rome), 3.

[9] Cf. Teresa Joseph, *Pope John Paul II as we remember him an Indian tribute* – Part 1 in *The Herald,* April 28-May 4, CXXXXII (2006) 17, 11.; *Pope John Paul II as we remember him an Indian tribute* Part II in *The Herald,* May 5-11, CXXXXII (2006) 18, 11.

encounters between believers of other religions that are taking place in various parts of the world. People all over the globe are aware of the importance of coming together and working together for peace and harmony.

A Journey to Assisi

An imaginary journey to Assisi, in the spirit of openness and dialogue, soon will supply sufficient thought for reflection and practical action. The very name of Assisi is filled with vibrations of peace. The peaceful atmosphere of Assisi, overflowing with sacred memories of St. Francis, challenges every pilgrim to a meaningful commitment to prayer, peace, reconciliation and harmony.

The day of prayer for peace on October 27, 1986, at Assisi, "offered the world a moving witness and was the prelude to historic change in the countries of Eastern Europe."[10] It continues to invite and challenge people of all religions. Assisi definitely marked the beginning of an extraordinary story in the history of religions. Today, in the Spirit of Assisi, members of the human family can dream of a new way of gathering. The way is new precisely because we have created space within our hearts to discover and appreciate believers of other religions. Again, it is new because we gather as brothers and sisters acknowledging and respecting each other's feelings and beliefs. It is ever new because we are ready to tune our hearts to listen to God who speaks in silence. It is new because there are a few common challenges that we can no more address only as individuals or as members of one single religious belonging. Today, there is a greater need for members of various religions to network together.

---

[10] Ufficio Delle Celebrazioni Liturgiche Del Sommo Pontefice (a cura), Together for Peace, Assisi, 24 January, 2002, Tipografia Vaticana, 2002, 14.

Assisi-One, was a prophetic gesture of Pope John Paul II. "Prayer is the bond which most effectively unites us: it is through prayer that believers meet one another" (John Paul II, message for the 1992 World Day of Peace). Change is possible only when believers meet in prayer; communicate with each other and plan together to set goals and work together to achieve them. Dialogue goes much beyond devising new visions and strategies. It takes us back to the essential core of our being; it touches our spirituality, our style of being and acting.

ASSISI - ONE	**ASSISI - TWO**	**ASSISI - THREE**
A prophetic gesture of John Paul II	9 January 1993	24 January 2002
27 October 1986, the first and most surprising convocation of religious leaders at Assisi.	Peace on the Balkans	"The first major world-involving event since the Twin Towers tragedy in New York" – Fides. Lamps of peace to light the future of humanity.

Assisi multicultural and multireligious is the most expressive image of the commitment of religions against every form of violence. On 27 October 1986, on 9 January 1993 and on 24 January 2002, Assisi became the "heart of a vast multitude of people calling for peace."

> "Young people of the third millennium, young Christians, young people of every religion, I ask you to be like Francis of Assisi, gentle and courageous 'guardians' of true peace based on justice and forgiveness, truth and mercy." – John Paul II

The Paradigmatic Metaphor of Assisi

Thanks to John Paul II, with the paradigmatic metaphor of Assisi, the Church, has offered a new icon to the World, the "Icon of Assisi". This was done with the participation of all world leaders.

> "Never again violence! Never again war! Never again terrorism! In the name of God, may every religion bring to the earth justice, peace, forgiveness, life and love" – John Paul II.

John Paul II has spoken eloquently on the Church's relationship with other religions: "The Church's relationship with the other religions is dictated by a twofold respect: 'Respect for man in his quest for answers to the deepest questions of his life, and respect for the action of the Spirit in man' " (RM n.29). This respect for the human person is based on theological anthropology. The Spirit of God blows freely, breathing life and love, and "the breath of the Spirit creates witnesses of peace." Encounter with believers of other religions is a very challenging task.

> Other Religions constitute a positive challenge for the Church: they stimulate her both to discover and acknowledge the signs of Christ's presence and of the working of the Spirit, as well as to examine more deeply her own identity and to bear witness to the fullness of Revelation which she has received for the good of all.[11]

Dynamic interaction with believers of other religions challenges the Church to discover and acknowledge the signs of Christ's presence and of the working of the Spirit. This indeed is a very delicate task. The person has to be fine-tuned to the rhythm of the Spirit. The Spirit blows freely, and a good amount of interior freedom is necessary to become aware of the working of the Spirit. The Church, the people of God, is a community of love and service. Her identity is refined and made perfect in the measure in which she confirms herself to her Lord and Master Jesus Christ. Among the various services that the Church makes available to people, there is one that is really challenging: "to

---

[11] John Paul II, Encyclical letter *Redemptoris Missio*, n.56.

bear witness to the fullness of Revelation which she has received for the good of all." Our neighbours, believers of other religions, want to hear the Good News of Jesus Christ. And we are duty bound to make it known to them in its fullness. That we carry out this task effectively and competently, there is need of an ongoing study and assimilation of the Word of God. We have to establish intimate relationship with Jesus through personal and community prayer and reception of the sacraments.

Our encounter with believers of other religions demands that we are well informed of our religion and that of others. True dialogue can take place only in a climate of genuine openness, mutual respect and reciprocal willingness to share the richness of each other's religion. Dialogue is an ongoing process.

St. Peter's Square Rome – A Replica of Assisi

The funeral of John Paul II provided a concrete opportunity for inter-religious dialogue and for meeting with the leaders of the great religions. Members of various religions gathered at St. Peter's Square, Rome, to pay their last tribute to the champion of dialogue. They came on their own. It was at the same Square that representatives of various religions pledged to unite to face challenges at the conclusion of the World Assembly of Religions (24-29 October 1999). John Paul II had shared with the participants the interest in dialogue among religions, which is one of the signs of hope.

> Moreover, the strength of witness lies in the fact that it is shared. It is a sign of hope that in many parts of the world interreligious associations have been established to promote joint reflection and action. In some places, religious leaders have been instrumental in mediating between warring parties. Elsewhere common cause is made to protect the unborn, to uphold the rights of women and children, and to

defend the innocent. I am convinced that the increased interest in dialogue between religions is one of the signs of hope present in the last part of this century (cf. *Tertio Millennio Adveniente*, 46). Yet there is a need to go further. Greater mutual esteem and growing trust must lead to still more effective and coordinated common action on behalf of the human family.[12]

Contemplation—the Power that Leads to Dialogue

Pope John Paul II was truly a champion of dialogue. The paradigm of Assisi, his unique gift to the world, is not merely just a theoretical expression. Examined in the light of his teachings and in the light of his own vast experience in dealing with people of good will of every culture and religion, it is evident that this paradigm is the fruit of a lived reality. In his Encyclical letter, *Redemptoris Missio* no. 91, the Pope courageously affirmed:

> My contact with representatives of the non-Christian spiritual traditions, particularly those of Asia, has confirmed me in the view that the future of mission depends to a great extent on contemplation.[13]

The Pope's words assumes greater significance when seen through the prism of "the terrestrial globe as a map of various religions" (Redemptor hominis, no. II). Contemplation has been identified as the professional secret for mission. Fixing our glance on Christ the Redeemer, assimilating his message and living a life congruent with the values of the Kingdom are all part of contemplation. It is to that unforgettable meeting of Assisi in 1986 that John Paul II returns to stress the common origin and common destiny of humanity:

---

[12] John Paul II, *Discorso del Santo Padre all'Assemblea Interreligiosa,* Piazza San Pietro, 28 ottobre 1999 in *http://www.vatican.va/holy father/ john paul ii/speeches/1999/october/documents/hf jp-ii spe 281 01999 inter-religious-assembly en.html,* n.4 (accessed on 4/4/2011).

[13] John Paul II, Encyclical letter *Redemptoris Missio* no. 91

Let me repeat here what I said at the end of that day of fasting and prayer:

The very fact that we have come to Assisi from various parts of the world is in itself a sign of this common path which humanity is called to tread. Either we learn to walk together in peace and harmony, or we drift apart and ruin ourselves and others. We hope that this pilgrimage to Assisi has taught us anew to be aware of the common origin and common destiny of humanity. Let us see in it an anticipation of what God would like the developing history of humanity to be: a fraternal journey in which we accompany one another toward the transcendent goal which he sets for us" (*Address at the Conclusion of the World Day of Prayer for Peace*, Assisi, 27 October 1986, 5).

Conclusion

What does acknowledging the paradigm of Assisis as John Paul II's unique gift to the world mean today? It means to feel the growing need to unite members of various religions to work together for love, peace and unity. It means to strengthen one's own religious identity. It is an invitation to become seekers of truth and enter into a dialogue with those whom we encounter. To carry out this dialogue effectively, each one needs to discern carefully in order to respect each other's identity without indulging in forms of syncretism.

It is up to us to create imaginary Assisis in every corner of our society. Time and again, we can and must proliferate the genuine experience of Assisi. Educational institutions are the prime places to pass on the precious paradigm of Assisi. We must remember that John Paul II was a Pontiff in dialogue with the young and their educators.

ASSISI A PRADIGMATIC METAPHOR

> The Church has offered a new icon, the "Icon of Assisi" with the participation of all the World leaders

ASSISI I

A Prophetic gesture of John Paul II

27th October 1986, the first and most surprising Convocation of religious leaders at Assisi

ASSISI 2
9th January 1993
Peace in the Balkans

ASSISI 3
24 January 2002

"The First major world-involving event since the Twin Towers tragedy in New York" -Fides

Lamps of peace to light the future of humanity

"Today, as on 27 October Assisi becomes once more the 'heart' of a vast multitude of people calling for peace".

" Young people of the Third Millennium, young Christians, young people of every religion, I ask you to be, like Francis of Assisi, gentle and courageous 'guardians' of true peace, based on justice and forgiveness, truth and mercy" ! John Paul II

Assisi multicultural and multireligious

Assisi is the most expressive image of the commitment of religious against every form of violence

"The breath of the Spirit creates witnesses of peace"

"We listen to the words, we listen to the wind. The wind is the Spirit, we listen to the Spirit"

John Paul II

"Never again violence! Never again war! Never again terrorism! In the name of God, may every religion bring to the earth justice, peace, forgiveness, life and love"
John Paul II

*"Through dialogue, the Church seeks to uncover the **'seeds of the Word'**, a **'ray of that truth which enlightens all men'**, these are found in individuals and in the religious traditions of mankind.*

*Other Religions constitute a positive challenge for the Church: they stimulate her both to **discover and acknowledge the signs of Christ's presence and of the working of the Spirit**, as well as to **examine more deeply her own identity and to bear witness to the fullness of Revelation which she has received for the good of all"** (Redemptoris Missio n.56).*

"The Church's relationship with the other religions is dictated by a twofold respect:

'Respect for man in his quest for answers to the deepest questions of his life, and respect for the action of the Spirit in man' " (Redemptoris Missio n.29).

CHAPTER FOUR

A Practical Approach to the Paradigm of Assisi

APPENDIX 1

In Profound Silence and in the Spirit of Prayer

Together with you, we wish to give the educators, or all those who are interested in this subject, a package of "profound silence and in the spirit of prayer." It may be mentioned that these are just simple guidelines and that you need to adapt the package for the age group of the participants. Experience in the field of education, especially in the field of religious pluralism, has taught us that when it is a question of approaching the "most precious treasures of other religions", we need to have prior education, specific sensibility and openness to "behold the truth" that believers of other religions hold dear. We, therefore, invite you to check out before the session whether your group is prepared to undertake this type of journey.

"In a world pervaded by audio-visual messages of every kind, it is necessary to restore zones of silence which allow God to make his voice heard and allow souls to understand and welcome his word." These words of John Paul II challenge us to create opportunities to taste the beauty of silence and to contemplate the richness of other religions. The purpose of this package is spelled out in the following objectives:

- To become aware that Assisi marked the beginning of an unforgettable story in the history of religions

- To move, in the Spirit of Assisi, towards a new way of gathering

- To discover the seeds of the Word present in other religions

- To get to know the Buddhist meditation to be acquainted with the seeds of the Word present in this religion

- To learn to "contemplate the seeds of the Word present in other religions"

- To pray together

Through a two-hour session, educators would be helped:

- To make an imaginary journey to "Assisi"

- To share their reflections, insights and commitment to create space within to discover and appreciate other religions

- To tune their hearts to listen to God who speaks in silence

- To enjoy a few moments of prayer together

You have two precious hours to make the group gradually enter into the contents of this package. We suggest one session and a moment of prayer.

SESSION 1

The Spirit of Assisi: Towards a New Way of Gathering Together

Time: 1 hr

Educator: Greets the group with a warm welcome and, if needed, offers a few minutes to the participants to introduce themselves. After creating a congenial atmosphere, the Educator presents the "introduction" given below.

Introduction

October 27, 1986, will forever remain as a memorable day in the history of humanity. On this unforgettable day, for the first time in history, representatives of religions gathered in Assisi to pray together.

Assisi is, no doubt, a landmark in the encounter of religions. This encounter assumes a profound meaning because it brings to light the other encounters that are taking place in various parts of the world between believers of other religions. Who can ever deny the intensity and richness of the daily personal encounters that are taking place in the most pluralistic societies?

In his apostolic letter, *Tertio Millennio Adveniente*, John Paul II announced that "the advent of a new millennium offers a great opportunity for interreligious dialogue and for meeting with the leaders of the great world religions" (TMA n.53).

Educator: Invites the participants to reflect on the following questions in silence:

Individual Work (*Time:3 minutes*)

- What do you suggest, in the Spirit of Assisi, for a new way of gathering together of believers of various religions?

- Drawing from your own experience of life, is it possible to discover the seeds of the Word in other religions?

- Do you have any practical suggestions to offer?

Educator: Invites the participants to gather in small groups (four participants in each group) and to share their answers. Each group is supposed to present the main points that emerged in this sharing.

Group Work *(Time: 5 minutes)*

Time for sharing in the assembly—Educator facilitates the sharing.

Educator: Makes a synthesis of what emerged from the sharing and moves on to developing the theme in the Spirit of Assisi for a new way of gathering together among believers of other religions.

Listening to Lived Experiences

The Reconciliation Walk

Given below is a courageous act through which the Christians asked forgiveness from Moslems for the actions of the soldiers in the Crusades 900 years ago.

On Easter Sunday morning in 1996, the Reconciliation Walk started from Cologne in Germany. It was 900 years ago that the first Crusade started at this very place. The report reads: A large group of Christians have started to march along the routes taken by the Crusade soldiers many years ago. They will travel along different routes, through former Yugoslavia, to reach Istanbul, Turkey, in the autumn. As they walk along the route, they will pray at different places and ask forgiveness from the Moslems that they meet for the actions of the soldiers in the Crusades 900 years ago.

Lynn Green, the leader of the march, reported: "As we walked, the highlight of the day was a visit to a Turkish Mosque and teaching centre in Cologne. The previous day, a local

Christian had contacted the Imam. He gave him a printed message of apology and asked if we could visit the Mosque.

"We were welcomed into a spacious room of prayer where about 200 men and boys gathered. The women and girls stayed in an adjoining room, but the Imam instructed them to read the message too.

"When everyone was settled on the carpet, the Imam welcomed us. Then I explained that we had come to apologise for the atrocities committed in the name of Christ during the Crusades. The reading of the message of apology in German, Turkish and English was greeted with loud sustained clapping.

"Then the Imam, who can speak all three languages, said, 'When I heard the nature of your message, I was astonished and filled with hope. I thought to myself, Whoever had this idea must have had an epiphany, a visit from God Himself. It is my wish that this project should become a very great success.'[1]

"Then he told me privately that many Muslims were beginning to examine their sins against Christians and Jews. He said that our example would show them how to act about the sins of the past. He promised to send the message out to their 250 Mosques in Europe."

Sarva-Dharma-Sammelana 1998 (National Inter-Faith Assembly on the Occasion of Yesu Krist Jayanti –2000)
"India is a land of many religions. Almost every second person whom we meet is different from us in his/her religious beliefs and practices. In such a religiously pluralistic society, encounter between various religions is unavoidable and even necessary

---

[1] *http://www.soon.org.uk/page15.htm* (the text of the apology also is available at this site).

at times. It is very common in our country that people belonging to one religious community invite the people of other religious communities to share their joy while celebrating their religious festivals and ceremonies. They exchange greetings and participate in common festive meal. Though they differ from one another in their approach to God and belief systems, they mutually accept and respect one another as persons. Here religion has become a means for unity and religious pluralism is understood and appreciated as 'unity in diversity'. In this context, dialogue among religions can certainly play a vital role in India. The need for such dialogue may be understood in three ways, namely, common origin, common journey and common goal."[2]

In the past years, India has witnessed a number of conflicts and tensions in the name of religion. In spite of this, there is still, in general, in many believers of various religions, the desire to journey together.

The National Interfaith Assembly was one of the major programmes envisaged in order to celebrate meaningfully the 2000th birth anniversary of Jesus Christ. Various programmes were undertaken for "self renewal and the renewal of relationship with the people of other faiths."[3]

Suggestions for follow-up action indicate concrete actions to be carried out at the grass-roots or district level, the State level and the national level and expectations from the CBCI Commission for Interreligious Dialogue. Given below are a few of them:

---

[2] Commission for Interreligious Dialogue Catholic Bishops' Conference of India, Sarva-dharma-sammelana 1998 (National Inter-Faith Assembly) *on the occasion of YESU KRIST Jayanti* –2000, A. Suresh (ed), New Delhi, 1998, 7.

[3] Sarva-Dharma-Sammelana 1998 (National Inter-Faith Assembly) on the occasion of Yesu Krist Jayanti –2000, 8-9.

- "Schools can organise inter-faith prayers during the morning assembly on important occasions. Introducing all religions in schools could be a part of value education

- Formation of harmony committees consisting of all religious leaders

- Promote a culture of tolerance and dialogue at all levels of life (Accept the identity of each religion and respect the differences.)

- Using mass media for promoting harmony in the state

- Inter-religious awareness should be brought out through television, radio and other mass media

- The meaning and the significance of all Religious Scriptures should be explained through mass media

- The CBCI Commission should continue its efforts and initiatives to promote Inter-Faith dialogue in India and organise more meetings for harmony among religions."[4]

Gladys June Staines

On the night of 22 January 1999, religious fanatics torched to death Graham Stuart Staines and his two sons, Philip (10 years) and Timothy (6 years) at Manoharpur, Orissa. The villagers found in the burnt station wagon three charred bodies sealed in embrace. This was shocking news. At this moment of immense pain, Gladys June Staines, moved by the spirit of Christ, was able to forgive the murderers of her dear ones.

> I have only one message for the people of India. I'm not bitter. Neither am I angry. I can forgive their killers' deeds. Only Jesus can forgive their sins. But they will have to ask. I have

---

[4] Sarva-Dharma-Sammelana 1998 (National Inter-Faith Assembly) 180-183.

one great desire that each citizen of this country should establish a personal relationship with Jesus Christ who gave His life for their sins. Every Indian should know that Jesus loves him or her, and in turn they should trust Him, and endeavour to love one another. Let us burn hatred... and spread the flame of Christ's love.[5]

This tragic event did bring together believers of various religions; given below is an extract from *The Times of India*.[6]

'Blessed are the peace makers; for they shall be called sons of God.' This is the thought that occurred to one as the Purushottam Express left the New Delhi platform with a batch of peace makers on a spiritual pilgrimage to Manoharpur in Orissa on Wednesday night. Manoharpur is the place where the Australian missionary Graham Staines and his two small children were burnt to death. 'We want to meet our Sister, Gladys Staines, who so graciously forgave her husband's killers and prayed that the Lord of Love must bless them too,' said Swami Agnivesh speaking on behalf of the multi-faith group at the railway station.

As the group[7] of around 60 men and women—Sikhs, Jains, Christians, Arya Samjists, Hindus, Buddhists and Muslims—stood in circles with lit candles and prayed before boarding the compartment, it marked the small beginning of a great journey to rouse the conscience of the nation over injustice

---

[5] V. Mangalwadi, Vijay Martis, M.B. Desai, Babu K. Verghese, Radha Samuel, *Burnt Alive The Staines and the God they loved*, GLS, Mumbai, 1999, 46.

[6] M. Kutty, *Blessed Are the Peacemakers* in *The Times of India*, 12 March 1999.

[7] "The delegation consisted of teachers and students of colleges and religious leaders. Jitender Kaur and Harminder Singh of Khalsa College, Swami Bhaktari Maharaj, Mohammad Rafique Quasmi of Jamaat-e-Islami Hind, Abdul Rashid Usmani of All India Muslim Majlis Mushawarat, Muni Manendra Kumar, Father George Koovackal, president of Messengers of Peace and Harmony, Jain Sadhvis and Catholic nuns were among the delegates."

and violence. (...) As Swami Agnivesh and other members spoke to a few newsmen present at the railway station it was evident that they were fired with a new zeal to mobilise people against injustices in society, oppression of the Dalits, ill-treatment meted out to women and exploitation of all kinds... .

Educator: Getting to know other religions is the key to the heart of joint collaboration. On another day, we will make a simple and humble effort to understand the Buddhist meditation and the Eucharistic celebration of the Catholics.

15 minutes of interval

SESSION II

Contemplate the Seeds of the Word Present in Other Religions

Courtesy Religion Teachers Journal[8]

Introduction

The sounds that reach our ears provide us with an enormous amount of information. They make us conscious of the voices of friends, the rustling of leaves, the crash of thunder, the roar of a lion, the bark of a dog, the chirp of a bird. Yes, noise and sound today have become almost part of daily living. Noise! We cannot escape it, even in some of our most remote areas. It is in the midst of noise that, deep within our being, we feel the need for silence.

---

[8] This moment of Prayer was already published in Religion Teachers Journal, March 2004 volume 38.2, 12-13. Permission for reprint received from Sue Cameron, Rights and Permissions, Twenty-Third Publications, through e mail message dated 28 March 2011.

Guided Imagery Meditation

Play soft music. The leader invites the group to take a comfortable position, to enter into a relaxed mood and to remain in this position for at least three minutes. He or she then asks the participants to reflect a while on the following:

Leader:

- Are you able to make peaceful, silent or quiet times for yourself?

- What relaxation techniques do you use to still your being? (Nature-walk, breathing exercise, music and so on). Still your mind and body as much as possible.

Let your mind take you to a peaceful place; for example, the seashore or a mountaintop.

- Depict by a symbolic drawing your experience during the exercise.

- In the stillness of your heart, what did your inner self say to you?

- Did God communicate any special message to you during the exercise?

The Desert

A symbol of inner silence

Silence as a condition for listening to God

This three-part exercise is meant to:

- Respect the need we all have to be alone.

- Help us listen to our inner self.

- Be in contact with God who speaks in silence.

Materials needed: Paper, coloured felt pens, crayons, poster paper, soft music and so on.

Reader One: It is a known fact that people often consider the "desert" as an ideal place for silence and interiority. Many Christians have loved and even gone to the desert. In the Holy Land, a person can visit the resting places carved on rocks by monks who lived there in solitude and silence.

Reader Two: Even today, there are people who live in such places with the same love and enthusiasm of the earlier monks. What is more amazing is that many of us have built a sort of desert within our own families; our rooms are transformed into places of silence. In the book of Hosea, we read: In the desert the Lord will speak words of love to his people. In the desert, God made his covenant with his people.

Leader: Let us now move to an imaginary desert.

- Can you dream of creating an imaginary desert within yourself? What does this desert look like? Draw a color picture that depicts your desert.

- In the rush of daily life, can you retire to this desert repeatedly?

- What can you gain by retiring to this desert?

Our relationship with God is simple and fascinating when we are really in touch with ourselves. Silence becomes new life in the Spirit, a space for God in us, a space to listen more attentively to his gentle voice: "I have called you by name...You are mine" (Isa. 43:1).

Group Prayer

Reader One: Friendship finds thousand ways of expressing itself. Praying together is one meaningful expression of deep friendship. The moments of silence during this prayer are purposely included so that we who are gathered together today may be intimately in the mystery we are celebrating.

Reader Two: In particular, silence favours listening to the Sacred Scripture and responding with meditation and prayer to welcome into our hearts the fullness of the voice of the Spirit and to unite personal prayer more closely with the Sacred Word. Fixed moments of silence are part of prayer and are meant to help us enter into ourselves and to respond to what we have listened to, or to praise and thank God in the depth of our being.

Reader Three: Aware of God's presence, let us prepare ourselves to "contemplate the seeds of the Word." (Pause for silence and soft music).

Reader Four: A reading from the gospel of Mathew 13:1-9 (the parable of the sower).

Leader: The following moments of silence will help us apply the message we have listened to in our own lives. This silence calls us to meditate briefly on what we have heard and to welcome into our hearts the fullness of the Word and of the voice of the Spirit. If you wish, you may write a personal prayer taking inspiration from the parable.

(Pause for silence accompanied by soft music).

The leader then invites the group to a few moments of spontaneous vocal prayer. This prayer springs from the Word and makes us more conscious of our "life hidden in Christ with God" (Col 3:3).

Exchange of Peace
Leader: Let us conclude this moment of prayer together with an exchange of peace: remembering our brothers and sisters all over the world.

Concluding Prayer
Leader: May peace and goodwill accompany us as we return to our daily commitments and may our life be an attentive

search with profound respect to each person to discover the seeds of the Word present in them, thanks to the presence and action of the Spirit.

All: Amen

APPENDIX II

The Educating Community Together for Building a Family of Truth

Note for the Educator

Together with you, we wish to offer a package on the following theme: "The educating community together for the building up of a 'family of truth.'" This packet is designed especially for every member of the educating community (educators, students, non-teaching staff and any person who is connected with school or college). Deep down in every human being, there is a thirst for truth. As seekers of truth, we can always share with others the fragments of truth that we have discovered. In a religious pluralistic context, this kind of sharing becomes privileged moments for growth.

The purpose of this package is spelled out in the following objectives:

- To explore what we mean by "Family of Truth"

- To understand the great religions of the world

- To question ourselves: Is it possible to pray together and, if so, how ?

- To become aware of the fact that the ministry of truth is an open journey

- To search the truth together in the educating community

- To become aware that new sensibilities need to be acquired in a rapidly changing religious world

- To learn the "when and how" of dialogue

Through a two-hour session, educators would be helped to:

- Deepen their commitment to search for the truth

- Find ways to enter more deeply into the heart of other religions

- Get to know experiment already tried out in schools

- Discuss points of common interest

- Enjoy a few moments of prayer together

You have two precious hours at hand to make the group to enter gradually into the contents of this package. We suggest one session and a moment of prayer.

SESSION (PART 1)

Seekers and Witnesses of Truth for a Meaningful Ministry of Truth

Time: 2 hrs with 15 minutes of interval in between the two moments

Educator: Greets the group with a warm welcome and, if needed, offers a few minutes to the participants to introduce themselves. After creating a congenial atmosphere, the Educator presents the "introduction" given below.

Introduction

"Once upon a time Truth went about the streets as naked as the day he was born. As a result, no one would let him into their home. Whenever people caught sight of him, they turned away or fled. One day when Truth was sadly wandering about, he came upon Parable. Now, Parable was dressed in splendid clothes of beautiful colours. And Parable, seeing Truth, said, 'Tell me, neighbour, what makes you look so sad?' Truth replied bitterly, 'Ah, brother, things are bad. Very bad. I'm old, very old, and no one wants to acknowledge me. No one wants anything to do with me.'

Hearing that, Parable said, 'People don't run away from you because you're old. I too am old. Very old. But the older I get, the better people like me. I'll tell you a secret: Everyone likes things to be disguised and prettied up a bit. Let me lend you some splendid clothes like mine, and you'll see that the very people who pushed you aside will invite you into their homes and be glad of your company.'

Truth took Parable's advice and put on the borrowed clothes. And from that time on, Truth and Parable have gone hand in hand and everyone loves them. They make a happy pair."[9]

Educator: Invites the participants to reflect in silence on the questions given below:

Time for Individual Work: 3 minutes

Questions for Reflection
1. What is the first thought that came to your mind as you listened to the conversation between Truth and Parable?

2. "Everyone likes things to be disguised and prettied up a bit." Is there a pinch of truth in this statement? What new insights does this statement offer you with regard to search for truth among believers of various religions?

---

[9] Weinreich Silverman B, *Yiddish Folktales,* trans. Leonard Wolf , New York, Schocken, 1988, 7 (as quoted by Susan M. Shaw, *Storytelling in Religious Education,* 381.

Educator: Invites the participants to gather in small groups (four participants in each group) and to share their answers. Each group is supposed to give a brief summary of the salient points that emerged in the sharing.

Time for Group Work: 5 minutes

Time for Sharing in the Assembly: 5 minutes

Educator facilitates the sharing

Educator: Makes a synthesis of what emerged from the sharing and moves on to develop the theme.

Seekers and Witnesses of Truth

Educator: Our spiritual patrimony is a heritage to be shared. "Together we can celebrate what is most sacred, precious, and singular in our scriptural faiths."[10] These words of Peter Ochs, the Edgar M. Bronfman Professor of Modern Jewish Studies, University of Virginia, give us a key to this session.

The experience of other educators and ours have offered us ample opportunities to experience how enriching educational experiences can be when mutual respect, open sharing and a genuine search for truth reigns in an educative ambient together with courageous efforts to apply new modalities of working. With this experience of the past and in the spirit of search together, we would like to focus our attention on entering into the dynamic of adoring the personal patrimony of each other. The educative directives cannot ignore the interiority of the person and his or her profound openness to the other. Education is a very complex reality. The beauty, the wonder and the marvel of each person and the entire

---

[10] *http://www.icjs.org/what/njsp/overvies.html* (accessed on 31/05/2001) Excerpts from the concluding chapter on *Christianity in Jewish Terms,* Westview Press, 2000.

cosmos need to be considered. Privileging the "way of wisdom", the sublime way cherished in the Bible and the traditions of various cultures, we will reflect on a few themes.

Encounters among religions are one of the strongest signs of our times. With a careful examination especially of the methodology used in these encounters, the sacred texts that inspired prayer, meditation and reflection efforts will be made to highlight possibilities that emerge from such encounters. Getting to know other religions is the key to the heart of joint collaboration.

What do we mean by Family of Truth?

It seems that the myth of secularisation is dying out and that religious revival is very much felt today. The plurality of cultures and religions is a sign of the growth of humanity. Plurality reflects the richness without measure of truth, and the design of God is to reconcile in Christ the multiplicity of things (Cf. EPh 1,10; Col 1,20).

To discover the common elements of truth for unified educative action, the educating community should know what we mean by "Family of Truth."

> 'Family of Truth': 'This concept reflects the affirmation of Vatican Council II on 'rays of truth' (NA2), the 'seeds of the Word' (AG11), 'All that is good and true that is found in them and is retained by the Church as preparation to welcome the Gospel' (LG 16), 'Feel' (with ecclesial sense) such seeds of truth signifies to build a 'Family of Truth.' While the 'hierarchy of truth' reflects the catechetical aspect, the 'Family of Truth' is inserted in the order of pre-evangelisation.[11]

---

[11] Michael Fuss, *Maria vincolo dell'unità nell'ecumenismo tra le religioni e di fronte ai nuovi movimenti*, in *Sette e Religioni* 3 (1993),117 note 6.

Truth is a gratuitous gift that God offers to every person. Every human being is looking for truth; the entire human family is on a constant journey in search of truth. Rino Fisichella affirms:

> The search for truth in fact, qualifies personal existence and permits to recognise a qualified denominator for dialogue among peoples"[12]

Building up a family of truth within an educating community requires a conscious feeling for and with other religions. In an educative ambient, where the integral formation of the person is taken care of and attention is focused on providing information and formation, feeling for and with other religions means to cross over from a mere informative knowledge of religions to enter gradually into the dynamics of getting to know what a believer of another religion holds dear. It means not just to know something on some practices, rites or celebrations of other religions but to make sincere attempts to learn more about the mystery that is being celebrated, the truth that spurs on the believers to continue their worship in that particular way and the joy and certainty they experience from such celebrations. It means to tune our being to perceive the transformative effects of such celebrations in the personal lives of the person, which no doubt overflows in his or her threefold relationship (other, self and others) and in his or her commitment towards common good. In the final analysis, the greatest challenge is to enter gradually into the rhythm of contemplation of those seeds of the Word that are present and active in the other. In this spirit, we will make an effort to understand Buddhist meditation today.

---

[12] R. Fisichella, Lezione inaugurale dell'anno accademico 1998-1999 dell'Ateneo Pontificio Regina Apostolorum, tenuta il 6 novembre 1998 *http://www.ateneo.org/ateneo/mof/fides et ratio una sfida .htm* (accessed on 06/11/2001).

Understanding Buddhist Meditation[13]

It is surprising to note that in Buddhism there isn't a term or word that can be translated into "meditation." What is more surprising is the fact that the entire life is a meditation for them. The word *bhavana* (cultivate/bring to maturation) is the word that expresses what in western language is called "meditation."

Buddhism has two forms of bhavana: *samutha bhavana* – concentrating on an object, an icon or an idea. It is more profound type of concentration; the mind enters into the contemplation of the reality. The originality of Buddhist meditation is *nirvana*, compassion. *Vipasyna* can be translated into intuition/interior vision/give attention. The last words of Buddha to the monks were: "Be attentive."

In Buddhism, there is a growing awareness: from natural things to one's own being, always moving ahead to more profound reality, with precision observing for example the joy one experiences and going further down to analyse from where that joy springs. The observation of the body leads the Buddhists to the awareness that nothing is permanent in our body, everything is in change. Here we can note that in Buddha there was already an anticipation of modern science. There isn't anything of which we can take pride. In pain, suffering, joy, in all this, we are not independent beings, we are included in a larger context. Man is not an autonomous figure.

The journey of purification and meditation: There are four steps in Buddhist meditation. It is like a gradual climbing. There is, of course, difficulty in climbing, but there is the joy of enjoying the fruits of those who have already meditated, this

---

[13] This is based on notes taken on 26.11.2001 during the course on Buddhism in dialogue with Christianity by Prof. Fuss Micheal, Gregorian University, Rome.

is a moment of rest, of courage to stand up and continue the journey; then comes the next moment with strength to continue the climb leading up to the final stage, abide, rest, with a deep desire to progress.

The dynamic behind this meditation is the courage to enter the current of life from this world to pass to the other (Here the Buddhists express an act of faith. In simple words, it means to say to Buddha that what you proposed is valid and I want to follow it...).

One who has begun the journey may feel well in the current of life and may gather the first fruits of his work. It can happen that one may doubt if he is able to make it to the end; in this case, he is free to return ...

One may not even return any more after halfway. The courage to face the rest of the journey has to come from within. The perfect man or the saint is the one who has completed the journey. It is always a point of greater perfection and not the point that is reached.

There are two strong moments: to undertake the journey and rest to start the journey again. There are different stages to be passed to reach *nirvana*. Passing through the various stages, meditation becomes always more and more part of one's being. In the first stage in the process of purification, the person is invited to cultivate positive elements (thought, reflection, ecstasy, deep concentration, equanimity, to be present, awake and attentive). This is a true mystical journey. "Rapture" — in psychology, we call it "peak experiences." In Buddhism, this means to go much more beyond till equanimity. The greatest mystery of Buddhist meditation lies in its openness, availability to empty self through a process of purification. The most important point is to remember that man makes use of different methods to purify himself better and more with the above-mentioned stages and with other means. *Nirvana* is a completely spontaneous and uncontrolled, unforeseen experience. It is a pure event. It can happen or not. But it is necessary that man commit himself to undertake the journey. In other words, there isn't a passage from the stages mentioned above to *Nirvana*. *Nirvana* is that total emptying of self, total openness. While the Buddhists don't say much on how *Nirvana* takes place, we need to welcome this reality, and contemplate the beauty of Buddhist meditation that overflows into service:

> The practice of meditation creates a climate of more profound silence that nourishes the attitude of compassion. Then this overflows in commitment and in action. These and other practices favour also those 'fruits of the spirit' — interior peace, joy, benevolence, serenity... that accompany an intense spiritual discipline.[14]

Another beautiful point of Buddhist meditation is that the one who practices meditation must become the divine abode. In the life of Buddha, this was made visible in the act of leaving his father's palace. As fruit of meditation, the one who meditates has to find the new house of virtue. Compassion is the supreme virtue in Buddhism. It means to share in the joys and sorrows of others, to sympathise with them, to manifest love, respect and equanimity.

You may have read in books that Buddhism is self-salvation. This is not true at all. As educating community, this simple journey into the Buddhist meditation gave us an opportunity to get to know something more. When you have an opportunity, you can pass on correct information about Buddhist meditation and *nirvana* to others.

Interval for 15 minutes

---

[14] Documento Domus Aurea *circa la presenza del Buddhismo* in *Europa* in *Pro Dialogo, Bulletin* 102, 1999/3, 341-345.

SESSION (PART 2)

For a Meaningful Ministry of Truth

Educator: Makes a synthesis of the first part of the session and leads the group to reflect together on the question: Is it possible to pray together and if so how to do it reflecting on the following experiences?

- Let us question ourselves: Is it possible to pray together and, if so, how?

Experience 1—Inter-religious Walk—Belgium

A friend of ours visited us from Belgium. On our way home from the airport, with great joy, this friend narrated to us a very touching experience of hers. A few days earlier, she had the joy of participating in an inter-religious walk invoking peace. To our question, how the moments of prayers were and who prepared the prayers, her answer was: "During the interreligious walk, the prayers were prepared by the representatives of the Church, Synagogue, and Mosque, etc., that we visited. When the group reached that particular place, after a short welcome, we were lead to prayer by the host group that welcomed us."

Experience 2—Prayers for Special Occasions—India

In India, students and teachers gather together to pray together on special occasions, such as the "opening of the School Year", "Children's Day", "Teacher's Day" and special "Feast Days." Mostly these moments of prayers are entrusted to a small group of persons who have a particular sensibility towards the believers of other religions. At times, there is one person or a small group that prepares the prayer that is published much in advance in magazines like *Awakening Faith*, *Kristu Jyoti*, etc., so that each school can adapt it to their particular context.

Experience 3—Inter-religious Prayers—Canada

The Canadian multi-faith schools have adopted a style of educating religiously "in ways which respect religious differences" not so much theoretically, as through examples. "Daily Readings/Prayers: The Toronto Model"[15] is yet another effort in this field. In the 1970s, the Toronto School Board considered the "problem of honouring Ontario regulations on opening exercises while respecting the religious diversity of the Toronto school population. The regulations call for the opening or closing of each school day "with religious exercises consisting of readings of the Scripture or other suitable readings and the repeating of the Lord's Prayer."[16] The Board soon noted that a change is called for in order to suit contemporary circumstances. A committee of around 35 people was formed under the leadership of Assistant Superintendent Ouida Wright by inviting all of Toronto's known religious bodies as well as a number of other potentially interested agencies to send representatives. It is reported that even the groups that did not participate expressed support for the undertaking and the wish to be informed of the outcome.

The first edition of the anthology was revised, enlarged and reissued in 1982. While we invite you to take some time to go through the various models of prayer proposed, it is worth remembering that:

> What emerges most significantly, however, are not the various ways in which the program falls short of its potential, but the fact that children and youth in Toronto's multi-faith schools are listening, thinking, appreciating, and are inwardly endorsing this aspect of their schooling which fosters their

---

[15] Donald J. Weeren, *Educating Religiously in the Multi-Faith School*, Calgary, Alberta, Detselig Enterprises Limited, 1986, 39-52.

[16] *Ibid.*, 39.

religious development. The possibility of enlarging the proportion of such students is inviting.[17]

Become Aware that Ministry of Truth is an Open Journey

As we journeyed together, we noticed that building up of a family of truth requires joint collaboration. The ministry of truth can be called an open journey. Truth opens horizons of friendship. We can say that truth is born from friendship. "A civic society is to be considered well-ordered, beneficial and in keeping with human dignity if it is grounded on truth" (Pacem in Terris, n.35).

> Different philosophical systems have lured people into believing that they are their own absolute master, able to decide their own destiny and future in complete autonomy, trusting only in themselves and their own powers. But this can never be the grandeur of the human being, who can find fulfilment only in choosing to enter the truth, to make a home under the shade of Wisdom and dwell there. Only within this horizon of truth will people understand their freedom in its fullness and their call to know and love God as the supreme realisation of their true self (FR 107).

The educating community in its search for truth needs to respect the freedom of each person. As John Paul II emphasises:

> Freedom has an inner 'logic' which distinguishes it and ennobles it: freedom is ordered to the truth, and is fulfilled in man's quest for truth and in man's living in the truth. Detached from the truth about the human person, freedom deteriorates into license in the lives of individuals, and, in political life, it becomes the caprice of the most powerful and the arrogance of power (Address to the Fiftieth General Assembly of the United Nations Organisation, 1995, n. 12).

> Consequently, the inseparable connection between truth and freedom which expresses the essential bond between God's

---

[17] *Ibid.,* 52.

wisdom and will is extremely significant for the life of persons in the socio-economic and socio-political sphere (Veritatis Splendor, n.99).

These words contain both a fundamental requirement and a warning: the requirement of an honest relationship with regard to truth as a condition for authentic freedom, and the warning to avoid every kind of illusory freedom, every superficial unilateral freedom, every freedom that fails to enter into the truth about man and the world (Redemptor Hominis, n.12).

It is in relation to objective truth that freedom of conscience finds its justification, inasmuch as it is a necessary condition for seeking truth worthy of man, and for adhering to that truth once it is sufficiently known (John Paul II World Day of Peace Message, 1991, n.1).

Educating Community

Prophets of Truth

- Courage to learn

- Courage to speak

- Courage to denounce (speak the truth in love).

"Away with falsehood then; let everyone speak out the truth to his neighbour; membership of the body binds us to one another" (Eph 4:25).

Seekers of Truth

- Each individual has a right to be respected in his or her own journey in search of the truth; there exists a prior moral obligation, and a grave one at that, to seek the truth and to adhere to it once it is known. (Veritatis Splendor, n.34).

- "It is only in freedom that man can turn to what is good" (GS, n.11).

- "You will know the truth and the truth will make you free" (John 8, 32).

New Sensibilities need to be Acquired in a Rapidly Changing Religious World

The field of religious pluralism is an open classroom. There is so much to be discovered as seekers of truth and there is so much to be made part of our very being. Here is just a word on new sensibilities to be acquired in a rapidly changing religious world. As prophets and seekers of truth, it is our duty to take time to check out our sensibility to our own religion and that of others.

How to be a Perfect Stranger

Openness to other people's religions often necessitates that we are informed about their celebrations. *"How to Be a Perfect Stranger is a Guide to Etiquette in Other People's Religious Ceremonies."*[18]

Both the volumes aim at offering the readers practical tips on the many what-to-do questions that crowd our minds when we are invited to participate in religious ceremonies or services that are not of our own tradition. The first volume provides practical guidelines to the basic service and ceremonies of all major religions and denominations in North America. The second volume offers guidelines and information for other religions and denominations in North America with smaller memberships. While both the volumes offer a large bit of information on the history and beliefs, the basic service, holy

---

[18] J. Arthur, & M. Stuart , (Editors) *How to Be a Perfect Stranger*, Vol. 1, *North America's Largest Faiths, A Guide to Etiquette in Other People's Religious Ceremonies*, United States, Skylight Paths Publishing, 1999, J. Arthur, & M. Stuart, (Editors) *How to Be a Perfect Stranger*, Vol. 2, *North America's Largest Faiths, A Guide to Etiquette in Other People's Religious Ceremonies*, United States, Skylight Paths Publishing, 1999.

days and festivals, life cycle events and home celebrations going down to details on attire, guest behaviour during and after the service, etc., it is left to each of us to discover what is at the "heart of the celebration."

Learn the When and How of Dialogue

A new religious mentality is being developed. As a result of this, quite a few reasonable questions are been raised. "When the Orthodox Chief Rabbi, Jonathan Sacks, wrote a book in 1994 entitled, *Will We Have Jewish Grandchildren?* it was not a rhetorical question, but a very real fear that Judaism might be in danger of disappearing."[19] In various educating communities today, there are children of mixed-faith marriages whose approach to religion is altogether different.

A supermarket of religions certainly offers a variety of choices. Precisely for this reason, there is a growing need today for a new group of educators who can accompany the educating community:

- To discover the depth and beauty of traditional religions

- To become aware of conflicting orientations and closed-up groups pretending to promise everlasting peace, joy and serenity

- To distinguish religious concepts from just a philosophical system of thought

- To build up a critical mentality that is capable of evaluating and discerning

- To distinguish between simple expressions and alternative system of thought

- To uphold what is true, good and beautiful in other religions

---

[19] J. Romain, *Your God shall be My God, Religious Conversion in Britain Today,* London, SCM Press, 2000, 11.

The most delicate task that the educating community is called to do is to learn the when and how of dialogue. The dynamic interaction that takes place within the educating community becomes the privileged moment for a meaningful dialogue of life.

Moment of Prayer

Educator: At the end of our reflection on the educating community for the building up of a "Family of Truth" — seekers and witnesses of truth for a meaningful ministry of truth— let us remain silent for a few moments.

Pause for silence and soft music

Reading of Evangelii Nuntiandi 78

> The preacher of the Gospel will therefore be a person who even at the price of personal renunciation and suffering always seeks the truth that he must transmit to others. He never betrays or hides truth out of a desire to please men, in order to astonish or to shock, nor for the sake of originality or a desire to make an impression. He does not refuse truth. He does not obscure revealed truth by being too idle to search for it, or for the sake of his own comfort, or out of fear. He does not neglect to study it. He serves it generously, without making it serve him.

> We are the pastors of the faithful people, and our pastoral service impels us to preserve, defend, and to communicate the truth regardless of the sacrifices that this involves. So many eminent and holy pastors have left us the example of this love of truth. In many cases, it was a heroic love. The God of truth expects us to be the vigilant defenders and devoted preachers of truth.[20]

Pause for silence and soft music

---

[20] Paolo VI, *Esortazione apostolica sull'evangelizzazione nel mondo contemporaneo: Evangelii Nuntiandi* (8 Dicember 1975).

Educator: Invites the participants to hold hands (if they wish) and pray in the stillness of their being for a while. This silent moment of prayer could be concluded by a symbolic offering of the participants' availability and desire to build a family of truth.

APPENDIX III

Beyond Religious Pluralism

Note for the Educator

The practical part that accompanies this work is intentional as there is a strong felt need and urgency to translate into practical action the well-defined theories and formulas available both in the Church and in society on dialogue between believers of various religions. We are indeed convinced that educators are in the best position to play a significant role as mediators in this delicate and diligent task. Certainly, each theme developed in this practical part is fruit of reflection and experience of our being and praying with believers of other religions. The driving force behind the work is therefore our belief that the rays of truth (*Nostra Aetate n. 2*) are present in other religions as well. So, we want to suggest a method and initiate a journey in the service of truth, to facilitate dialogue and mutual listening among believers of other religions in order to create a new mentality: to begin to "contemplate the seeds of the Word present in other religions" and to do it as a "Family of Truth."

It is evident that we have no pretensions to offer readymade instant solutions or well-defined conclusions. We are all seekers of truth and companions on the journey. The task of drawing up conclusion falls on each person in his or her openness to search the truth and to dwell in it.

Here is our final open-ended session on the theme, "Beyond Religious Pluralism."

This packet is especially designed for every member of the educating community (educators, students, non-teaching staff and any person who is connected with school or college).

The purpose of this package is spelled out in the following objectives:

- Become aware that it is a religious man or woman who lets the face of a religion to shine out

- Get in touch with one or two persons who have made an effort to understand another religious tradition

- Become aware of the fact that we need to be bilingual to enter the true spirit of dialogue

- "Share the treasures of faith in a new dialogical language"

- Keep the doors of our hearts open and to feel free to enter into dialogue with the "Family of Truth"

Through a two-hour session and a moment of prayer, the participants will be offered a chance to:

- Go a step beyond their own religion

- Get to know Buddhadasa and his programme for inter-religious dialogue

- Search one's proper religious tradition to discover persons who have made efforts to understand or enter into dialogue with other religious traditions

- Become aware of the linguistic demands in sharing one's faith

- Get a glimpse of what it means to "share the treasures of faith in a new dialogical language"

- Enjoy a few moments of prayer in the company of Mary, friend of humanity

SESSION (PART 1)

Beyond Religious Pluralism

Time: 2 hrs, with 15 minutes of interval in between the two sessions

Educator: Greets the group with a warm welcome and, if needed, offers a few minutes for the participants to introduce themselves. After creating a congenial atmosphere, the Educator invites the group to enter into this session with an open heart.

Introduction

Educator: Introduces the session by writing the following sentence on the board:

"Behind every religion there is the religious man of all times and of all civilisations."[21]

After a minute of silence, the educator asks the participants to discuss the following questions:

1. What is the first thought that came to your mind when you read the above sentence?

2. If behind every religion "there is the religious man of all times and of all civilisations" what practical consequence this statement can offer us to learn the truths of other religions?

Educator: Invites the participants to gather in small groups (four participants in each group) and to share their answers. Each group is supposed to give a brief summary of the salient points that emerged in the sharing.

---

[21] J. Delumeau, (a cura) *Il Fatto Religioso*, Torino, Società Editrice Internazionale, 1997, XI.

Time for Group Work: (5 minutes) At the end of the group discussion, each group is asked to prepare a chart highlighting two main points that emerged during the discussion. (Chart paper and sketch pens will be made available).

Each group is asked to put up their poster in the hall.

Once each group has put up their poster, the educator solicits the whole group to take a glance at the poster. This work needs to be done in perfect silence. Each participant is asked to write down the points that he or she may consider important for discussion in the assembly. When all have finished writing, the educator takes into consideration the three main points that emerged and elaborates them in the assembly. These three points will serve as connecting link to the following point: to get to know Buddhadasa[22] and his effort to promote inter-religious programmes.

It is those men and women behind every religion who in one way or another have mediated the knowledge of one's own religion and that of other religions. Conscious of who they are and what their religious beliefs are, different people have made courageous efforts to study, reflect, get to know and voice their opinion regarding other religions.

Today, in the spirit of profound respect, we shall consider one such person: Buddhadasa[23] Indapanno.

---

[22] This part on Buddhadasa is elaborated basing on the following: Fuss M., *Cristo nel moderno pensiero religioso non-biblico* MO2076, Università Gregoriana, 2002, also notes taken during lessons on 18.2.2002 and 25.2.2002.

[23] Buddhadasa was born on 27 May 1906 at Bumrieng, in Thailand. Right from his early age, he was in contact with children from Muslim families. This helped him to understand that "committed, virtuous and spiritual persons can be found also outside Buddhism." Besides a good basic intellectual formation, he had experience of work in the family shop, especially after the death of his father. The contacts he had with western technicians settled in Thailand offered him

Buddhadasa is a great patriarch—brought true renewal within Buddhism—and is one of the Buddhists who have written most on Christ.

Openness to Other Religions

Buddhadasa introduced a new spirit of openness to other religions in the monastery that he founded. Surprising to note that he made available in the monastery different images of various religions for the monks to use as objects of their meditation. They also chanted hymns of other religions. Undoubtedly, this openness was the fruit of his personal inspiration.

Dramatic Representations to Make Known the Spirit of Other Religions

Buddhadasa organised dramatic representations to make known the spirit of other religions in an appealing manner to a wider audience. The scope of such theatrical representations was to enter into the spirit of other religions.

He also promoted inter-religious programmes for his monks. Thanks to his openness to inter-religious dialogue, he soon realised that there was need for a "new language" for

---

possibilities to be open to other parts of the world. He committed himself to a constant discovery of Buddhism. To return to the original message of Buddha, he searched in the sacred texts, especially in *Tripitaka* without passing through the comments and other books. As a result of all this, he decided to create a quiet place in order to "verify and deepen the doctrine" that he had learned. He decided to live a life that is "transparent, extremely independent, to search now onwards purity and truth [...] from now on we will not follow the world [...] we will live in it physically, but, spiritually, we will make it the best possibly independent, to find purity [...] we will do like Buddha." It is said that for all his life, he tried his best to conform himself to this programme, which he described in one of his letters to his brother (*Un Buddista parla del Cristianesimo ai Buddisti* (traduzione di Francesco Caponi), Milano, Paoline, 1990, 10-11).

dialogue among believers of various religions. This is easily understandable today, as we know how many different meanings certain common terms have in various contexts and within various religions. Terminological difficulty today is a known fact. The new language Buddhadasa proposed is known as the "language of Dharma."

The Language of Dharma

To understand what the "language of Dharma" is, we need to go deep into "experience" and "mystery." According to Buddhadasa, each one needs to use his or her own terminology that comes from mystery. This could be explained better by an example. If one of us needs to use the word "God", one needs to do so not under a dogmatic key but drawing intensely from one's experience that is fruit of prayer, meditation, contemplation, etc. As we know, God is far beyond dogma and so going beyond dogmatic boundaries, we may be able to enter into the language of our God experience. In the same way, read the experience of Dharma. Dharma is the universal and cosmic reality; it is the entire message of Buddha; it is the sacred word; it is the sacred environment; it is all that is sacred; it is mystery. Buddhadasa affirmed that in dialogue, each dialogue partner should be faithful to one's own terminology that is fruit of experience as we have mentioned above. Understood in this way, words or terms would never become a cage of defense but means to communicate the rich experiences of the sacred mysteries each of our religions hold dear. What we have in communion no doubt is our fundamental experience of faith. Spurred on by this experience of faith, let us take a few moments to consider the word "life." Life means different things to different people. To a person who considers the word "life" outside a religious context, it means to enjoy life. Seen in the context of religions, "life" is illusion. True life is life beyond, life eternal, life offered by God. In this way, for the

Buddhists true life is life in *Nirvana*. In this paradox, we need to explain the terminology of Dharma.

Understanding Religions in the Light of Experience

Religions ought to be understood in the light of experience. The experience of love, joy and suffering shared with others. From personal subjective experience is born a community. We can transfer this very same logic to a religious experience. Looking at the first group of disciples of Jesus, we can say that there are twelve persons who have shared and believed in the experience of Jesus the Lord. Looking at the five disciples who followed Buddha, we can affirm that they have shared and believed in the experience of Siddharta's illumination. In both the above-mentioned cases, "experience" is at the basis and remains as the starting point. It is from the experience narrated that the community of believers and followers is formed. We can say that experience is the principal normative dimension.

In the light of experience, Buddhadasa proposes that Christians and Buddhists can interpret the experience of suffering. Christians can interpret suffering in the light of Christ and his total surrender to the Father. The Buddhists can interpret suffering in the light of Buddha completely abandoned to Nirvana, to emptiness.

Buddhadasa and the Cross of Christ

Moving from an anthropological vision of Christ, Buddhadasa explains the cross of Christ. He begins with the single individual person and affirms that it is necessary to purify ego or self = "I". He proposes that we need to cancel the "I" = (+) and thus we have the cross. To cancel ego, self, "I" is the central message of Buddhism. To find salvation, man needs to cancel ego; this way man finds nirvana. According to Buddhadasa, the symbol of the cross is the summary of the entire Buddhist doctrine. He had a very fascinating philosophy of life, which is summarised in the following words of his: "My personal emptiness is wisdom, my fullness is emptiness." His letterhead carried this expression. According to Buddhadasa, when we let go of our "I", we are no more egoists. It is a gradual passing through death to arrive at complete freedom. For him emptying is complete expression of intelligence. We have to be reborn=nirvana/life eternal. At the heart of this message is the non-attachment that shines out in the life of Buddha and Jesus. Moved with compassion, they rendered humble service to others. Buddhadasa emphasises that this attitude of humility — emptiness lets the barriers to fall off and in this, there is the basis for dialogue. It is evident that for him dialogue initiates from an existential basis of life—a life of humility and openness. Having humility as the starting point, Christians can explain what Christ means for them and Buddhists can narrate what Buddha stands for in the Buddhist tradition. Only in such an attitude of humility, we will be progressively able to move on to Christology and Buddhology—in concrete terms, to the crucifixion of Christ and to the illumination of Buddha.

A Pedagogy of True Humility and Love

At the basis of genuine dialogue, there ought to be a pedagogy of true humility and friendship. In such a climate, there will certainly be a profound search for truth, space to welcome criticisms and to clarify them if needed. Learning from each other and the service of truth carried out in love will enhance such type of dialogue. Buddha gave his teaching. Jesus gave his life. From this shared spirituality of gradual passing from death to life and to a life of witness, Buddhadasa has developed a programme of intense collaboration and witness. He quotes the Gospel text where Jesus kneels down to wash the feet of his disciples (John 13, 1-15) as a symbol of humble service of Buddhists to the poor. It is important to note the shift from an existential experience to a diakonia of service towards the world. Both Christianity and Buddhism believe in translating spiritual experience into a diakonia of service. Here the beauty of dialogue blossoms into witness of life (Cf. RM n. 56)[24] expressed in concrete gestures. The spiritual experience of Buddha – illumination and the spiritual experience of Christ – incarnation, passion, death and resurrection become the motivating force that prompts both Buddhists and Christians to believe in this type of a dialogue of life weaved together in love and friendship. Thailand is famous for the so-called "committed Buddhism." Today, in different parts of the world, Buddhists have various initiatives in the field of education and other services in collaboration with Christians, Muslims and others.

The Challenge to be Bilingual

In his stimulating contribution to 2 Kings chapters 18 and 19, Brueggemann affirms that the Christian community bearer of a message of liberation must be bilingual. Diakonia of truth as a new style of approach to inter-religious dialogue challenges us personally and as educating communities to be bilingual. There is need for a language to be used within the same community of believers and at the same time greater need for another language that is capable of communicating with believers of other religions. Our spiritual experience has to speak to the myths of that particular religion and to that

---

[24] *Redemptoris Missio* n.56 clearly states that "Those engaged in this dialogue must be consistent with their own religious traditions and convictions, and be open to understanding those of the other party without pretence or close-mindedness, but with truth, humility and frankness, knowing that dialogue can enrich each side. There must be no abandonment of principles nor false irenicism, but instead a witness given and received for mutual advancement on the road of religious inquiry and experience, and at the same time for the elimination of prejudice, intolerance and misunderstandings. Dialogue leads to inner purification and conversion which, if pursued with docility to the Holy Spirit, will be spiritually fruitful."

particular group of people. Here then is the urgent need to develop within our community of believers a new language that is the fruit of a genuine search for the rays of truth present in religions. It has to be a language that respects the freedom of each human person, a language that is aimed at promoting a "culture of life" and a "Family of Truth."

"Share the treasures of faith in a new dialogical language"

The "Family of Truth" needs to be alert to the ever-growing interest that humanity at large manifests to the person of Jesus. Persons like Buddhadasa and others who have taken care to get to know Jesus remaining in their own religious tradition, invite the Christian community to share Christ in a new way, to discover and to contemplate the richness of the Christian faith allowing a new dimension of contemplation to take root in our communities and in our personal lives. If we are convinced of the "rays of truth" present in the other religions, then we need to fix our contemplative gaze on those rays of truth or on those treasures and contemplate Christ, the Lord of life. It is a call to discover new richness of our faith; it is an invitation to recognise how others perceive Christ. When we are at this point of respectful acceptance and profound contemplation, yes, then and then only we will be in a position to understand others and to let exchanges of dialogue grow and blossom. Love, esteem and dialogue go hand in hand and are sustained by uninterrupted contemplation.

> The mission, considered as dynamic presence of the Word incarnate, is realised through the invitation of Jesus to contemplation as contemplation is realised in sharing the treasures of faith in a new dialogical language.[25]

---

[25] Michael Fuss, *"Contemplatio in missione". L'ambito buddhista della missione ad gentes* in M. Rostkowski (ed.), *La missione senza confini, Missionari Oblati di Maria Immacolata, Roma 2000*, 233-248.

Believers of various religions, aware of their religious identity and at the same time open to the treasures of other religions, can in total respect join hands and unite the best of efforts "for a common witness of the supreme values."[26]

By entering into a new dynamic of contemplation and dancing to the rhythm of the Spirit who progressively guides humanity "to all the truth" (John 16, 13) we can commit ourselves evermore consciously as "partner" in humanity's shared struggle to arrive at truth; and to make visible the "diakonia of the truth."[27] Educators can accompany the educating community in the most delicate task of discovering the true image of every man and woman, making him or her aware of the proper rights and duties and respect them. Religious freedom of every single person and the divine design regarding religions need to be kept in mind.

> The different ways in which God, acting in history, cares for the world and for mankind are not mutually exclusive; on the contrary, they support each other and intersect. They have their origin and goal in the eternal, wise and loving counsel

---

[26] *Ibid.*, 246.

[27] *Fides et Ratio* n.2. The Church is no stranger to this journey of discovery, nor could she ever be. From the moment when, through the Paschal Mystery, she received the gift of the ultimate truth about human life, the Church has made her pilgrim way along the paths of the world to proclaim that Jesus Christ is "the way, and the truth, and the life" (*Jn* 14:6). It is her duty to serve humanity in different ways, but one way in particular imposes a responsibility of a quite special kind: the *diakonia of the truth.* (1) This mission on the one hand makes the believing community a partner in humanity's shared struggle to arrive at truth; (2) and on the other hand it obliges the believing community to proclaim the certitudes arrived at, albeit with a sense that every truth attained is but a step towards that fullness of truth which will appear with the final Revelation of God: "For now we see in a mirror dimly, but then face to face. Now I know in part; then I shall understand fully" (*1 Cor* 13:12).

> whereby God predestines men and women "to be conformed
> to the image of his Son" (*Rom* 8:29). God's plan poses no threat
> to man's genuine freedom; on the contrary, the acceptance of
> God's plan is the only way to affirm that freedom (*Veritatis*
> *Splendor n.45*).

An inter-religious anthropology needs to be carefully and critically studied and gradually developed. Schools and Universities can play a significant role in giving birth to such anthropology. Prof. Fuss synthesises the unique role of inter-religious anthropology:

> In as much as comparative discipline, inter-religious
> anthropology studies, first of all, the other religious
> expressions as such, in order afterwards to explore the proper
> faith in dialogue with this enriching experience. At this point
> the 'inter-religious dialogy' would have realised its scope:
> having passed from the intuition of faith of other to the
> inevitable spiritual confrontation, respecting from one side
> the dynamic of religious freedom, while on the other side,
> nourishing the proper faith and confronting, Christians and
> non, with the call to reconciliation and personal conversion.[28]

Prayer is at the heart of every religion. Prayer[29] has found its expression in many ways: from a simple invocation to praise, thanks and contemplation. Dialogue among believers of various religions can lead to prayer. Believers from various parts of the world have repeatedly requested for moments of inter-religious prayer. Just to quote one voice: "I long for the only dialogue which will help me to realise more deeply the Mystery of the Spirit in me."[30]

---

[28] Michael Fuss, *"Pellegrina fra Pellegrini". La reciproca diaconia di Teologia e Antropologia delle Religioni*, in M. Crociata (a cura di), *Teologia delle religioni. Bilanci e prospettive*, Milano, Paoline, 2001, 262-63.

[29] The Catechism of the Catholic Church in part four offers a very valid and beautiful contribution to Christian prayer; see 613-688.

[30] R Murray, *'Dialogue Postponed'*, in *Asia Focus*, 1970, 211-210.

Speaking of the various religious traditions of Asia, the Asian bishops have highlighted the importance of dialogue of prayer. According to them, sustained and meditative dialogue with the members of various religions in prayer can reveal to us what the Spirit has taught to others and to express it in a marvelous variety of ways.[31]

Dynamic interaction between believers of various religions in a dialogical spirit spurs on to new horizons of contemplation; one such is to "consider the faithful of other religions though remaining in their diversity, reciprocally guests in the conscience of one's own faith."[32]

Educator: Invites the participants to reflect on this point for a while.

(Pause for 2-3 minutes of silence followed by an interval of 15 minutes)

---

[31] Cf. Office of Ecumenical and Interreligious Affairs, FABC, *Dialogue Resource Manual for Catholics in Asia*, FABC-OEIA, 2001, 91.

[32] Michael Fuss, *"Contemplatio in missione"* 244.

Moments of Prayer with Mary, Friend of Humanity and 'Icon of Dialogue'

Materials needed: Soft music, an oil lamp, a light to focus on the image of Mary, a flower pot, an icon or a frame of Mary or the pieta of Michel Angelo.

The prayer will take place in a semi-dark room or hall. The participants will be seated in a semicircle and the icon or image of Mary will be placed in the middle of the circle.

Guide: Invites the participants to take a comfortable position. The atmosphere in this semi-dark hall and the soft music will help the participants to create a spirit of silence and recollection within. Different people are drawn to Mary. Poets have sung her praises, artists have depicted her in a thousand ways and writers have produced volumes in her name. Millions and millions of Catholics and believers of other religions have offered and continue to offer their homage to her, visiting her shrines and standing in silence before her image.

Voice: United with all our brothers and sisters who regard Mary as their friend and companion on life's journey, we are gathered here today around Mary. The lighted lamp and the flowerpot we are about to place before Mary are our expression of love and gratitude to her.

(Two representatives will carry forward the lighted lamp and the flowerpot and place them in front of Mary).

(Soft music and pause for silent reflection)

Guide: We shall spend a few moments in listening to a few experiences to recall how Mary accompanies different people on their life's journey.

(Soft music and pause for silent reflection)

Voice 1: In the city of Bombay in India, there is a Church at Mahim. Every Wednesday evening, there is a special Marian Moment followed by the Eucharistic celebration in that Church. Every Wednesday, at Mahim, there is a large crowd of Catholics and believers of other religions (some even take leave from work to be present for the celebration) who come together for prayer. Quite many who participate in the celebration say, "We find peace; we receive strength from Mary to go ahead in our daily life. We feel her presence close. This is what brings us to this Church and to this time with Mary."

Voice 2: The importance of Mary in favouring dialogue among believers of various religions is quite well recognised today. Mary's "yes" in the salvific dialogue between God and humanity, her openness and her total availability to give everything to her Son are worth mentioning. Representations of Mary with symbols of other religions are in circulation in various parts of the world.

Mary's humility and her lowliness offer valid suggestions to present-day man and woman on how to welcome and contemplate the Greatness of the Other. The song of Magnificat (Luke 1, 46-55) is a song of thanks to God Almighty. We too, like Mary, can become aware of the great things that the Almighty is accomplishing for us and sing his praises.

Guide: It will be very enlightening to see how Mary is presented in the sacred texts of a few religions. Who is Mary? How does the sacred text of the Muslims present her?

Voice 3: "Mary is mentioned 34 times in the Qu'ran, the only woman mentioned by name, and Islam pays Mary its highest compliments, namely that she is a person of faith and of submission to God, a model to be imitated by all Muslims. The Qu'ran is very clear that Mary was born without sin. In some parts of the Middle East, Muslims, particularly women, visit Marian shrines to seek her intercession. Otto Meinadus, who lived in Egypt for several years, describes some of the ways in which a common devotion to the Virgin Mary serves as a bridge between Muslims and Christians"[1]

Guide: Who is Mary? How do the Sacred texts of the Catholics present her? Today we shall focus our attention on Mary at the foot of the Cross.

Voice 4: According to the Catholic tradition, Mary played a unique role in the saving history of humanity. Through her total availability and her wholehearted collaboration she co-operated with God for the incarnation of Jesus (Cf. Luke 1, 26-38). Faced with things that were beyond her understanding, she questioned and trusted in what was told to her. In fact, Evangelist Luke uses a beautiful expression to indicate Mary's capacity to meditate and contemplate: "She kept all those things in her heart" (Cf. Luke 2, 51). The Gospels record that on two occasions, moved by compassion; she extended her service to those in need. The first fact occurred when she came to know that her cousin Elizabeth in her old age had conceived a child (Luke 1, 36-56). Mary remained with Elizabeth for about three months. The second was at a marriage at Cana in Galilee. Mary noticed that wine was running short and she informed her Son Jesus that "they have no wine" and she told the servants "Do whatever He (Jesus) tells you" (John 2, 1-11).

Guide: Mary's ability to face suffering and her courage to believe that suffering is not the end but there is a way in suffering have struck many. To cite an example, we were taught that "many Buddhists are moved to tears seeing Michelangelo's *Pieta*—the supreme emblem of suffering." Mary's acceptance of suffering has become a valid point for dialogue among believers of various religions, precisely because human life is so closely signed by suffering, pain and sorrow.

Voice: Mary made herself available to the action of the Spirit. We can say that her entire life is availability to the Spirit. Mary is an icon of the Spirit. Redemptoris Mater[2] in n.24 expresses it powerfully:

> We see the Apostles before the day of Pentecost 'continuing with one mind in prayer with the women and Mary the mother of Jesus, and with his brethren' (Acts 1:14). We see Mary prayerfully imploring the gift of the Spirit, who had already overshadowed her in the Annunciation (51).

And so, in the redemptive economy of grace, brought about through the action of the Holy Spirit, there is a unique correspondence between the moment of the Incarnation of the Word and the moment of the birth of the Church. The person who links these two moments is Mary: Mary at Nazareth and Mary in the Upper Room at Jerusalem. In both cases, her discreet yet essential presence indicates the path of "birth from the Holy Spirit." Thus, she who is present in the mystery of Christ as Mother becomes—by the will of the Son and the power of the Holy Spirit—present in the mystery of the Church. In the Church too, she continues to be a maternal presence, as is shown by the words spoken from the Cross: "Woman, behold your son!..."Behold, your mother." (Redemptoris Mater n.24).

Guide: "We listen to the words, we listen to the wind. The wind is the Spirit: we listen to the Spirit." This impromptu statement that came from John Paul II during the inter-religious meeting for peace in the lower square of Assisi (January 24, 2002) could be true also of this our gathering together around Mary. The Spirit is talking to us as persons and as a group. Let us now listen to a reading taken from the Gospel of St. John. Mary faces the most crucial moment of suffering.

> Near the cross of Jesus stood his mother, his mother's sister, Mary the wife of Clopas, and Mary Magdalene. When Jesus saw his mother there, and the disciple whom he loved standing nearby, he said to his mother, 'Dear woman, here is your son,' and to the disciple, 'Here is your mother.' From that time on, this disciple took her into his home (John 19, 25-27).

Guide: (Invites the participants to a moment of silent prayer). Let us in the stillness of our heart speak to Mary

(Pause for silent prayer)

Guide: On Calvary, along with Jesus, Mary also experienced crucifixion. The pain and agony of the Mother was no less than that of the Son. In Mary, we see the love of a mother for her only son and for all human beings whose mother she was called to become. She accepted it all as part of the package she received from the Father when she accepted to be the mother of the Saviour.

(Pause for silent prayer)

Guide: Let us bring to our mind every man and woman who lets the face of a religion shine out. Let us unite ourselves with every human person of good will who is in search of truth, joy, peace and love. Let us remember with gratitude those who have made efforts to learn and understand the truth of other religions and continue to do so.

(Pause for silent prayer)

Guide: Let us ask Mary, friend of humanity, to be with us in our effort to welcome the sorrows and pains of life, in our commitment to find a suitable language to share the treasures of our faith, in our desire to strengthen our religious identity, in our readiness to contemplate the seeds of the Word present in other religions and in our joint efforts to build a family of truth.

(Pause for silent prayer)

The guide may invite the participants to intervene with any other prayer they may desire.

Guide: As we conclude this moment of our prayer, may joy and peace be with us as we continue our commitment to go beyond religious pluralism to discover the rays of truth present in other religions. And may Mary be our friend and guide and may she help us to face the challenges and difficulties of day-to-day life.

Bibliography

Alberich Emilio, *Pluralism* in *Dizionario di Scienze dell'Educazione* (a.c. di Josè Manuel Prellezo (coord.) Carlo Nanni, Guglielmo Malizia), Torino, ELLE DI CI, 1997.

Alberich Emilio, Binz Ambroise, *Adulti e Catechesi*, collana Studi e ricerche di catechetica, ELLE DI CI, 1993.

Amaladoss Michael, *Identity and Harmony Challenges to Mission in South Asia* (Conference, Sedos Missionary Congress, 3-8 April 2000, Rome).

Anonymous, *The Cloud of Unknowing*, trans, Clifton Wolters, Baltimore: Penguin, 1961.

Astley J., *"Faith Development: An overview"*, in Astley J., and Francis L., (Ed), *Christian Perspectives on Faith Development*, Michigan, William B. Eerdmans publishing company. 1992.

Benedict XVI, *Pope John Paul II My Beloved Predecessor*, Bombay, Pauline Publications, 2007.

Beversluis J. (ed.). *A Sourcebook for Earth's Community of Religions.* Grand Rapids, MI:CoNexus 1995.

Bissoli Cesare, *Il Papa interpreta il sistema educativo di don Bosco*, Leumann (Torino), ELLEDICI, 2000.

Braham P. Gupta, *Children's Literature and Value Education* in Indian Currents, November 2, 1992, vol.4.

Brueggmann Walter, *Living Toward a Vision: Biblical Reflections on Shalom*, New York, United Church Press, 1982.

Buber M., I *racconti di Chassidim*, Milano, 1945.

Camps Arnulf, *Partners in Dialogue (translated from the Dutch by John Drury)*, New York, Orbis Books Maryknoll, 1983.

Cantwell W, *The meaning and end of religion*, Mineapolis: Fortress press, 1991.

Commission for Inter-religious Dialogue Catholic Bishops' Conference of India, *Sarva-Dharma-Sammelana 19998 (National Inter-Faith Assembly) on the occasion of YESU KRIST Jayanti –2000*, A. Suresh (ed), New Delhi, 1998.

Congregation for the Clergy, *General directory for catechesis*, Vatican City, Libreria Editrice Vaticana, 1997.

Currents in World Christianity (CWC) *Newsletter* 3 (November 2001).

David NG, *Holy People in a Holy Creation*, in Norma H. Thompson (ed) *Religious pluralism and religious education*, Birmingham, REP, 1988.

David Tracy, *The Analogical Imagination: Christian Theology and the Culture of Pluralism*, New York, Crossroads, 1981.

Dawe G. Donald, '*Religious Pluralism and the Church*', in *Journal of Ecumenical Studies* 18 (Fall, 1981).

Delumeau Jean (a cura) *Il Fatto Religioso*, Torino, Società Editrice Internazionale, 1997.

Diocesan Catechetical Centre, *Awakening Faith*, Bandra, Mumbai. (1996-2002).

Documento Domus Aurea *circa la presenza del Buddhismo in Europa* in *Pro Dialogo, Bulletin 102, 1999/3.*

Erikson Erik and Erikson J., *The power of the newborn* in Mademoiselle, 62 (1953).

Erikson Erik, *Gandhi's Truth: On the Origins of Militant Nonviolence*, New York, W.W. Norton, 1975.

________ , *Identity and the Life Cycle*, New York, Norton, 1959.

Fontana Umberto, *Relazione, segreto di Ogni educazione*, Leumann (Torino) ELLEDICI, 2000.

Fore William F., *Television and Religion,: The Shaping of Faith, Values, and Culture*, Minneapolis, Asgsburg Publishing House, 1987.

Fowler James, 'The Enlightenment and Faith Development Theory', in *Journal of Empirical Theology, 1(1988).*

________ , *Faith, liberation and Human Development: three Lectures* in The Foundation, 1969.

__________ , *Toward a Developmental Perspective on Faith, in Religious Education*, 1974.

__________ , *Weaving the New Creation: Stages of Faith and the Public Church*, San Francisco, Harper & Row, 1991.

__________ , *Faith Development and Pastoral Care*. New York, Fortress 1987.

__________ , *Stages of Faith: The Psychology of Human Development and the Quest for Meaning*, San Francisco, Harper & Row, 1981.

FOX M., *The Coming of the Cosmic Christ*, San Francisco, Harper & Row, 1988.

Arinze Francis, *World Religions: Join Hands To Face Challenges!* (Opening address to World Assembly of Religions, Vatican City, 25th October 1999)

Fuss Michael, *Il fenomeno della nuova religiosità in Europa Una sfida pastorale*, in *Sette e Religioni* 2 (1992).

__________ , *Maria vincolo dell'unità nell'ecumenismo tra le religioni e di fronte ai nuovi movimenti*, in *Sette e Religioni* 3 (1993).

__________ , *New Religious Movements*, in *Following Christ in Mission. A Foundational Course in Missiology, Sebastian Karotemprel (Ed)*, Philippines, Daughters of St. Paul, 1996.

__________ , Nuovi Salvatori per i tempi nuovi? La ricerca di salvezza nella nuova religiosità in Piero Coda (a cura) L'Unico e i molti. La salvezza in Gesù Cristo e la sfida del pluralismo, Roma, Mursia- Pontificia Università Lateranese, 1997.

__________ , *Il ritorno del religioso: e la Chiesa?*, in Sette e Religioni nel mondo 4, 1 (1998).

__________ , *"Contemplatio in missione". L'ambito buddhista della missione ad gentes* in M. Rostkowski (ed.), *La missione senza confini, Missionari Oblati di Maria Immacolata, Roma 2000*.

__________ , *Formazione al dialogo interreligioso e tra le religioni* -**MS2103** (materiale) *Università Gregoriana, 2000-2001*.

__________ , *"Pellegrina fra Pellegrini". La reciproca diaconia di Terologia e Antropologia delle Religioni*, in M. Crociata (a cura di), Teologia delle religioni. Bilanci e prospettive, Milano, Paoline, 2001.

__________ , *Buddhismo e cristianesimo: 2 paradigmi e le loro omologie in Il buddismo dottrinale* in *dialogo con il cristianesimo* (dispensa) Univerisità Gregoriana, 2001/2002.

__________ , *Cristo nel moderno pensiero religioso non-biblico* MO2076, (dispensa) Università Gregoriana, 2001-2002.

__________ , *"Diaconia alla verità": l'atteggiamento pastorale nei confronti degli orientamenti conflittuali* MS2110 (materiale) *Università Gregoriana, 2001-2002.*

__________ , *La sfida degli orientamenti conflittuali,* (MO2B51 dispensa) Università Gregoriana, 2001-2002.

__________ , MS2110 *"Diaconia alla verità": l'atteggiamento pastorale nei confronti degli orientamenti conflittuali,* Università Gregoriana, Roma, 2001-2002.

__________ , *New Age, I: il mercato di una nuova spiritualità* MO2A59 (dispensa) Università Gregoriana, 2001-2002.

__________ , Unità e pluralismo delle forme dell'esperienza di Dio. Nella prospettiva della fenomenologia delle religioni, in Associazione Teologica Italiana, Maurizio Aliotta (a cura) Cristianesimo, religione, religioni. Unità e pluralismo dell'esperienza di Dio alle soglie del terzo millennio, Milano, San Paolo, 1999.

Galante Joseph A, Lost in Prayer, in http://batr.org/view/040405.html

Gianetto Ubaldo, *Aspetti E Problemi dell'Educazione Cristiana in Atto,* in *L'Educazione Cristiana negli insegnamenti degli ultimi Pontefici da Pio XI a Giovanni Paolo II, Norberto Galli (a cura)* , Milano, *Vita E Pensiero, 1992.*

Genovese Elizabeth Fox, *The Legacy of John Paul II. Why the bishop of Rome may be the most important figure in this secularistic age* in *http://www.ctlibrary.com/268* (accessed on 12/4/2005).

Hayes Patrick J., *Rules of Thumb for Reading Church Documents, in* The Living Light, Spring 2001.

Inter-religious Assembly, 25-28 October 1999, Vatican City, *Final report,* in pp. 14-16; in *Pro Dialogo,* Bulletin 103, 2000/1.

John Paul II , *Redemptoris Mater* (25 March 1987).

__________ , *Redemptoris Missio* (7 December 1990).

__________ , *Centesimus Annus (1 May 1991).*

__________ , World Day of Peace Message, 1991

__________ , *Veritatis Splendor* (6 August 1993).

__________ , *Tertio Millennio Adveniente (10 November 1994)*

__________ , Apostolic Exhortation, *Ecclesia in Asia*, Vatican City, Editrice Vaticana., 1994.

__________ , Letter of to Rev. Egidio Viganò Rector Major of the Society of S. Francis de Sales in the centenary year of the death of St. John Bosco, Rome 31 January 1988. in *Insegnamenti di GIOVANNI PAOLO II*, XI, I, Libreria Editrice Vaticana, 1998.

__________ , *General Audience, Wednesday 9 September 1998*

__________ , General Audience, Wednesday 29 March 2000.

__________ , Message to the Youth of the World on the occasion of the XVI World Youth Day *http://www.vatican.va/holy father/ john_paul_ii/messages/youth/documents/hf jp-ii mes 20010215 xvi-world-youth-dayen.html the VII World Youth Day http://www. vatican.va/holy father/john paul ii /messages/youth/index.htm (accessed on 24/3/2011).*

__________ , Message for the VII World Youth Day *http://www. vatican.va/ holy father/john paul ii /messages/youth/index.htm* (accessed on 24/ 3/2011).

__________ , Message for the XIII World Youth Day 1997 *http://www. vatican.va/holy father/ john paul ii/messages/youth/index.htm* (accessed on 24/3/2011).

__________ , Message to the Youth of the World on the occasion of the XVII World Youth Day (Toronto 18-28 July 2002). *http://www. vatican.va/holy father/john paul ii/messages/youth/index.htm* (accessed on 9/1/2002).

__________ , Omelia di Giovanni Paolo II per l'inizio del Pontificato, Domenica, 22 ottobre 1978 in *http://www.vatican.va/holy_father/ john paul ii/speeches/1978/documents/hf jp-ii spe 19781022 inizio-pontificato it.html* (accessed on 8/3/2011).

__________ , *Fides et Ratio* (14 September 1998).

__________ , *Novo Millennio Ineunte* (6 January 2001).

__________ , Discorso del Santo Padre all'Assemblea Interreligiosa, Piazza San Pietro, 28 ottobre 1999 in *http:// www.vatican.va/holy*

father/john paul ii/ speeches/1999/october/documents/hf jp-ii spe 281 01999 inter-religious-assembly en.html, n.4 (accessed on 18/4/ 2005).

________ , Last Will and Testament. Official English Translation of Pope John Paul II Last Will and Testament VATICAN, April 7, 2005 (LifeSiteNews.com) - The translation from Italian into English has been done by the Vatican Information Service: http:/ /www.lifesite.net/ldn/2005/apr/05040703.html (accessed on 16/ 4/2005).

________ , Concerning pilgrimage to the places linked to the History of Salvation, in *http:// www.vatican.va/holy father/john paul ii/ letters/documents/hf jp-ii let 30061999 pilgrimage en.html*

________ , Apostolic Letter, Rosarium Virginis Mariae, 16 October, 2002.

________ , Master in Faith, Apostolic Letter Of His Holiness John Paul II To The Very Reverend Father Felipe Sainz De Baranda Superior General of the Order of the Discalced Brothers of the Blessed Virgin Mary of Mount Carmel on the occasion of the IV centenary of the death of Saint John of the Cross, Doctor of the Church, n.4 in *http://www.ewtn.com/library/ Papaldoc/ Jpmaster.htm* Master in Faith, n.2.

________ , Apostolic Constitution Universi Dominici Gregis On the Vacancy of the Apostolic See and the Election of the Roman Pontiff, in *http://www.vatican.va/holy father/john paul ii/ apost constitutions/documents/hf jp-ii apc 22021996 universi-dominici-gregis en.html* (accessed on 14/4/2005).

________ , Papal Bull Incarnationis Mysterium n.7. in *http:// www.vatican.va/jubilee 2000/ docs/documents/hf jp-ii doc 30111998 bolla-jubilee en.html* (accessed on 8/4/2005).

________ , Apostolic Exhortation, *Ecclesia in Asia* (6 November 1999) n. 1-51, in Insegnamenti di Giovanni Paolo II, 22/2, Città del Vaticano, Libreria Editrice Vaticana, 2002.

________ , Orientale Lumen (to mark the Centenary of Orientalium Dignitas of Pope Leo XIII in *http://www.vatican.va/holy father/ john paul ii/apost letters/documents/hf jp-ii apl 02051995 orientale-lumen en.ml*

__________ , Last Will and Testament. Official English Translation of Pope John Paul II Last Will and Testament VATICAN, April 7, 2005 (LifeSiteNews.com) - Following is the text of the spiritual testament of John Paul II, which was released today in an Italian translation of the original Polish. The translation from Italian into English has been done by the Vatican Information Service: *http://www.lifesite.net/ldn/2005/apr/05040703.html*

Joseph T., *Family of Truth: The Liminal Context of Inter-Religious Dialogue An Anthropological and Pedagogical Enquiry*, ISPCK, Delhi, 2009.

__________ , Contemplate the Seeds of the Word *in Religion Teachers Journal*, March 2004 volume 38.2, 12-13.

__________ , *Pope John Paul II as we remember him an Indian tribute* – Part 1 in *The Herald*, April 28-May 4, CXXXXII (2006) 17, 11.; *Pope John Paul II as we remember him an Indian tribute* – Part II in *The Herald*, May 5-11, CXXXXII (2006) 18, 11

Add also mine KJC and Examiner

Julián Herranz, The Pope has shown the evangelizing power of a mystic, Interview in El Pais (with Enric González) in *http://www.opusdei.org/art.php?w=32&p=6565* (accessed on 11/5/2005).

Knitter Paul F., *No other name*, SCM Press Ltd., London 1985.

Lattin Don, Fimrit E Peter, Chronicle Staff Writers, in San Francisco Chronicle *http://sfgate.com/cgi-bin/article.cgi?file=/c/a/2005/04/02/MNGB3C2BBC1.DTL* (accessed on 8/5/2005).

Lee James Michael, *The Shape of Religious Instruction, A Social Science Approach*, Mishwaka, REP, 1971.

__________ , The Flow of Religious Instruction, Mishwaka, Indiana, REP, 1973.

__________ , *The Content of Religious Instruction* , Birmingham, REP, *1985*

__________ , *The Blessings of Religious Pluralism* in Norma H. Thompson (ed) *Religious pluralism and religious education*, Birmingham, REP, 1988.

__________ , (ed) *Handbook of Faith, Birmingham, REP, 1990.*

__________ , *The Sacrament Of Teaching, volume 1, getting ready to enact the sacrament: a personal Testament, a social science approach*, Birmingham, Alabama, Religious Education Press 1999.

L'Osservatore Romano, *Un pellegrinaggio universale per dire grazie al Pellegrino*, Mercoledì 6 aprile 2005.

L'Osservatore Romano, Giovedì 7 aprile 2005, 1.

MAGIDA Arthur J. & Stuart M. Matlins (Editers) *How to Be a Perfect Stranger*, Vol. 1, North America's Largest Faiths, A Guide to Etiquette in Other People's Religious Ceremonies, United States, SkylLight Paths Publishing, 1999.

__________ , *How to Be a Perfect Stranger*, Vol. 2, North America's Largest Faiths, A Guide to Etiquette in Other Peoples's Religious Ceremonies, United States, Sky Light Paths Publishing, 1999.

Maier H., '*Erikson's Developmental Theory*' in Thomas M., (Ed), *The Encyclopedia of Human Development and Education : Theory, Research and Studies*, Pergamon Press, New York 1990.

Mangalwadi, Vishal, Vijay Martis, M.B. Desai, Babu K. Verghese, Radha Samuel, *Burnt Alive The Staines and the God they loved*, GLS, Mumbai, 1999

Marian Studies, *Marian Spirituality and Interreligious Dialogue*, Annual Publication of the Mariological Society of America, Vol.XLVII 1996, The Marian Library, University of Dayton.

Martini Carlo Maria, *L'Evangelizzatore in San Luca*, Milano, Ancora, 2000.

Mattei Giampaolo, *L'ultimo e più grande Viaggio Apostolico di Giovanni Paolo II sulla Rotta di Dio* in *L'Osservatore Romano*, Mercoledì 6 aprile 2005, 3.

Miller Donald, "*Religious Education and Cultural Pluralism,*" in *Religious Education* 744 (July-August, 1979).

Moran Gabriel, *Religious Pluralism: A U.S. and Roman Catholic View* in Norma H. Thompson (ed) *Religious pluralism and religious education*, Birmingham, REP, 1988.

Motto Francesco, *Un sistema educativa sempre attuale*, Leumann (Torino), ELLEDICI, 2000.

Nanni C., Educazione in *Dizionario di Scienze dell'Educazione* (a.c. di Josè Manuel Prellezo (coord.) Carlo Nanni, Guglielmo Malizia), Torino, ELLE DI CI, 1997.

Office of Eccumenical and Interreligious Affairs, FABC, *Dialogue Resource Manual for Catholics in Asia, FABC-OEIA*, 2001.

Paolo VI, *Esortazione apostolica sull'evangelizzazione nel mondo contemporaneo: Evangelii Nuntiandi* (8 dicembre 1975).

Pollo Mario, *Le sfide educative dei giovani d'oggi,* Leumann (Torino) ELLEDICI, 2000.

Pontifical Council for Promoting Christian Unity, *Directory for the Application of the Principles and Norms of Ecumenism, Boston, St. Paul Books & Media,* 1994.

Pontificia Università Gregoriana, Facoltà di Missiologia, *programma degli studi,* 2001-2002.

Prellezo J.M., *Storia della scuola* in *Dizionario di Scienze dell'Educazione* (a.c. di Josè Manuel Prellezo (coord.) Carlo Nanni, Guglielmo Malizia), Torino, ELLE DI CI, 1997.

Pushparajan A. (Ed) *Challenges to Religious Pluralism, The commission for dialogue,* Madurai, 1994.

Ratzinger Joseph, Homily at John Paul II's funeral Mass on April 8, 2005 in St. Peter's Square in Zenit.org (accessed on23/3/2011). [Original text in Italian; translation issued by Holy See] ZE05040802.

Romain J., *Your God Shall Be My God - Religious Conversion In Britain Today,* London, SCM press, 2000.

Russo Adolfo, *Religioni in Dialogo,* Napoli, Edizioni Scientifiche Italiane, 2001.

Sachidanand Acharya John, *A New Curriculum Framework for Value Education,* in *Paths to a New Value Education,* Indian Catechetical Association, Herve Morissette (Editor), Bangalore, St. Paul's Press, 2001.

Sarti Silvano, *Crescita e orientamento,* Roma, LAS, 1992.

Scott Kieran, *Review of forging a better religious education in the third millennium,* in *The Living Light,* Winter 2000, Vol. 37-n°2.

Shaw M.Susan, *Storytelling* in *Religious Education,* Birmingham, Alabama, Religious Education Press, 1999.

Shockley Grants., *Religious Pluralism and Religious Education: A Black Protestant Perspective* in Norma H. Thompson (ed) *Religious Pluralism and Religious Education,* Birmingham, REP, 1988.

Streib Heinz, *Mass Media, Myth and Narrative Religious Education,* in British Journal of Religious Education, XX,1, 1997.

Sullivan Lawrence E., *Victor Turner*, 1920-1983 in History of Religions 24 (1984) 2, 163.

Thompson H. Norma (ed) *Religious pluralism and religious education,* Birmingham, REP, 1988.

Tonelli R.,. Gallo L., Pollo M., *Narrare per Aiutare a Vivere, Narrazione e pastorale giovanile,* Torino, ELLE DI CI, 1992, p 155. Buber M., I racconti di Chassidim, Milano, 1945.

Trenti, Zelindo, *Educare alla fede – saggio di pedagogia religiosa,* Elledici, Leumann (Torino) 2000.

Turner Victor, Turner Edith, *Image and Pilgrimage in Christian Culture, Anthropological perspectives,* New York, Columbia University Press, 1978.

Turner Victor, *Ritual, Tribal and Catholic,* in *Worship* 50 (1976) 508.

__________ , *Symbols and Social Experience in Religious Ritual* in *Studio Missionalia* 23 (1974), 10.

Ufficio Delle Celebrazioni Liturgiche Del Sommo Pontefice (a cura), *Together for Peace, Assisi,* 24 January, 2002, Tipografia Vaticana, 2002, 14.

Vatican Council II, *Declaration on religious freedom Dignitatis humanae* (7 December 1965).

__________ , *'Declaration on the Church's relation to Non-Christian Religions Nostra aetate'* (28 October, 1965) .

Webster D., *James Fowler's Theory of Faith Development",* in *British Journal of Religious Education, 7(1984).*

Weeren Donald J., *Educating Religiously in the Multi-Faith School,* Calgary, Alberta, Detselig Enterprises Limited, 1986.

Young Bong Oh and Sun Young Park, *Buddhist Education and Religious Pluralism* in Norma H. Thompson (ed) *Religious pluralism and religious education,* Birmingham, REP, 1988.

www.ingramcontent.com/pod-product-compliance
Lightning Source LLC
LaVergne TN
LVHW090007180726
843489LV00001B/422